Dear Daughter

what I wish I'd known at your age

by
Roy Sheppard

centre

First published in 2013 by
Centre Publishing,
Croft House, Clapton, Radstock, Bath,
Somerset, BA3 4EB England.
Tel: 00 +44 (0) 1761 414541
Fax: 00 +44 (0) 1761 412615
Email: info@TheSensibleUncle.com
Web: www.TheSensibleUncle.com

Paperback: ISBN 978-1901 534-221
Book cover design by Roy Sheppard.
Front and back cover photographs © Peter Simonson 2013
Cover models: Kari and Kylie Sellers
Book design Antony Parselle

Kind regards

table of contents

introduction

As a young woman in the 21st century, you are part of a generation of the best-educated, the most intelligent, street-smart, savvy and sexy women who have ever lived. Even if you might not feel as though you are part of any of the above right now, at no time in history have there been so many opportunities for women in a growing number of countries and cultures to excel at whatever they choose to do with their life.

Feminists in the 1960s loudly proclaimed that women could have it all. However, that part of feminism has proven to be untrue. You *will* have to make choices.

Your future as a successful, fulfilled woman will be based on your personal priorities and choices. And will become the result of all the decisions you make (and don't make) in the years to come. Therefore your ability to make great decisions is key to this. The best decisions are always made using the most up-to-date and relevant information available to you. Crucially, you have to be open to that information in order to be fully responsible for the consequences of your ultimate decisions. This book is designed to help you make better choices. To give you an 'edge' on life.

Think back to when you were fourteen. How much more did you know about 'life' than when you were just ten? And at eighteen, how much more than when you were fourteen? Twenty-two now? Thirty? And in the next four years, you will know even more about yourself and life than you do today. And so on. Based on that reasoning, how much more do women of forty, fifty, sixty or seventy know about being a woman? Here is a unique chance to learn from their mistakes... and their wisdom.

guidebook for your life journey

Every year millions of young people set off with their rucksacks to see the world. New people, new cultures and totally new experiences. In almost every case, these travellers have life-changing experiences they carry with them for the rest of their lives. Even the most experienced travellers know that a travel guide for their particular destination is an essential part of their 'kit'. An up-to-date guidebook to tell you the best ways to get around, where to stay, what to see, where to party and how to be safe, perhaps in areas of the world with wildly different customs and attitudes towards women. In some places, you really need to know stuff before you get there.

But does studying and learning from a travel guide spoil the spontaneity and enjoyment of the travel experience? No way. You stand to gain far more by being better informed.

It's exactly the same with this book. Think of it as a travel guide for your future life as a woman. Throughout, you'll find nuggets of wisdom to help you on your way.

Some truly amazing women have contributed; collectively, there are more than one thousand five hundred years of life experience. There's also input from quite a few switched-on men, too. These people don't know you. Therefore they have no agenda. They are not trying to control or patronise you. They have simply volunteered their time to look back on their own lives and share what they have learned on their own journeys.

It's been said that our minds are like parachutes. They only work when they're open. So, are you open to learning aspects about life that you have yet to experience from kind people who have been there ahead of you? If so, keep reading.

For about ten years I worked on BBC TV and radio as a presenter and reporter. It was drummed into you by producers, *"Engage your brain before putting your mouth into motion."* A thoughtless comment would instantly be heard by millions. A minor mistake just makes you look stupid. The wrong sentence or even the wrong word has the potential to end your career. Therefore, you learned to think before you spoke. It's a good idea to adopt this approach to your own life.

You are finally taking your own path after years of what may have felt like totally unnecessary 'supervision'. Now, at long last you can do what you like, with whomever you like, without the knowledge or approval of 'overprotective' parents. It's both exciting and a bit scary. And it should be.

Wanting to cut your mother's apron strings in order to be more independent is perfectly natural. But be aware that this coincides with a very real identity crisis for many mothers. They are now faced with who they will become once their 'little girl' leaves the 'nest'. In many cases, a woman's identity is so wrapped up in her role as a mother that she may fear becoming completely redundant, that the bond so carefully nurtured with you over the years is about to be broken. It is about to change, but it doesn't necessarily have to get broken as you transition into being a woman.

And as for fathers, they remember very clearly how preoccupied they were with girls when they were your age. And how they were prepared to say and do just about anything in order to get a girl into bed. Their male teenage sexual experiences, occasional reckless behaviour and irresponsibility, not to mention their fantasies and dreams, have turned into nightmares now that they are the protective fathers of young women.

building bridges

It might be helpful to think of parents, step-parents and extended family members as 'hands'. Some children grow up with these hands wrapped around them, sharing the role of supporting, nurturing, protecting, guiding, occasionally punishing and repeatedly dipping into their pockets to pay for everything. Sometimes though, the daughter only has one of those hands to provide for all her needs. And in other cases she grows up without any helpful hands available to her at all.

Whoever may have handed this book to you cares deeply about your well-being and future happiness. They know that you are entering the next stage of your life. They know you need to assert your independence and are prepared to step back to give you the space to do so. Your needs are being taken seriously (whether you are aware of it or not). You will certainly encounter situations and experiences that are new to you. Stubbornly insisting that you do everything on your own is not always a sensible idea. Part of being a mature person is knowing when to ask for help.

I hope this book provides you with invaluable practical help, but also acts like a bridge between parents and daughters. Ask anyone who knows how bridges are built and they will tell you they are always constructed from both sides simultaneously. Refusing to collaborate with parents on the opposite shore will simply make it unnecessarily difficult for you to build that bridge on solid foundations.

So dip in and out of this book. Let it help you see the bigger picture of your future life. Discuss the topics with your girlfriends. And ask your parents about their lives before you were born, what they have learned about life, their fondest memories and the lessons they have learned. Ask them what they agree about in the book. By talking, you might all learn something from the conversations and each other.

Roy Sheppard, Bath, England, February 2013

what I wish I'd known about:

being a woman

How would you define the main differences between being a girl and a woman? How confident are you that your response would come close to an answer from a thirty-year-old or a seventy-year-old woman?

Jennifer is in her fifties and observed that the main difference between girls and women is that girls tend to be self-obsessed about what they look like, and what others think about them based on who they are on the 'outside'. Older women in her view become far more self-aware, and at peace with whom they evolve into being on the 'inside'. Such women have developed a deep sense of 'knowing' about life, without feeling the need to take centre stage by articulating their wisdom.

growing pains

Talk to almost any intelligent, mature woman and she'll admit that her early life as a woman was about pretending to be how she thought a woman should behave, think and look like. As for her emotions, they were forever changing and routinely intense. It was a normal day to experience the full range, from feeling deliriously happy to believing the world was about to end following a disagreement with a friend or family member.

Much of the time she felt awkward, uncertain, confused, frustrated, angry, resentful and completely misunderstood – with not enough doors at home to slam. It's also likely she felt that she was routinely 'patronised', treated like an idiot, and constantly controlled by totally unreasonable parents who had no idea what her life was like. On top of that, she'd add that no one ever took her views seriously (especially at home). Whilst at school she felt surrounded by jerks, losers and girls who were capable of levels of cruelty that were difficult to comprehend. Recognise any of these feelings?

While trying to figure out everything, most young women become brilliant at putting on a 'front'. Everyone feels the need to look as if they know what's going on. The vast majority of young men and women don't. It's all about appearance and attitude. Some manage better than others to fool everyone into believing that they've got it all sorted – but it's a hard act.

Dear Daughter
It's actually more cool to not care about 'being cool'.

Jessica Drummond is an expert on health for young women (www.JessicaDrummond.com):

> *"What women of my generation heard is that we must be all things to all people. We must be brilliant career women, we must be finger-painting and cookie baking mothers, we must be tall, thin, young, gorgeous wives, and we must do it all flawlessly without any assistance, or we are simply not enough. What I wish I had known before I tried for many years to do all of these things flawlessly, is that I am already enough.*
>
> *"I wish I had better understood the delicate, strong, and uniquely feminine body that I am living in, and how to take great care of it... so I could have more pleasurably taken hold of all of the opportunity that is now available to Western women.*
>
> *"My best advice for young women today is to understand your body, how to take care of it, then live in it and use it's feminine capacity to step out into the world and make your own*

choices about which amazing opportunities you will take. You are already beautiful, and you are already enough. So, simply follow the path that feels the most fun because when your body is strong and your work is fun, you will be giving all of us your best gifts."

Lisa Bahar (LisaBahar.com), a licensed marriage and family therapist, who works with a lot of adolescent girls and young adults adds this:

"It is one of the most challenging times in life being a teen, and yet it is the very time to explore who you are and who you are not. Follow your own inner guidance or wise mind. Follow your 'gut' or that funny feeling that tells you to do something (including not going to a certain event or being with certain people). It is what many term 'following your heart'. This is what will take you through life and help you feel that you are 'on the right track'.

"If you are by chance a little different, rest assured you will most likely not fit in, but that does not mean you are not good enough or less than anyone else. Be true to yourself, and those that are meant to be with you will gravitate to you with no effort. Just don't busy yourself with those that judge you. Or decide to not enjoy and understand you.

"Learn to have a sense of humour about being a woman in today's world, sometimes seeking advice from a grandmother or a trusted female elder who will listen to you and perhaps provide guidance as you explore and learn more about yourself and who you are. My mother believed in true love, romance and was genuine with her desire to be loved for who she was. Enjoy the love in the packages it comes in, and don't settle due to peer pressure.

"Resist any sense of urgency to get married because everyone else is or because you don't want to be alone. Wait for what you want. Accept that it may not come in the way you think. There is plenty of love out there to give and receive in a variety of ways.

"Enjoy being a woman. Be confident. Be smart and educate yourself. Be gracious and, most of all, be kind daily to those around you. Say I love you when you feel the instinct. Smile."

Kate Sturgess (KateSturgess.com), is a former model:

*"Realise that there's no such thing as perfection in life. I've learnt to forgive myself for not being perfect. When I was young everything was terribly, terribly important. It was at the time. But looking back it really wasn't. My mother often repeated the quote by writer Ray Bradbury. It's **so** true. 'Life is like falling off the top of a skyscraper and growing your wings on the way down.'"*

You've probably already lost count of the number of times you've been asked: *"What do you want to be when you grow up?"* But have you ever been asked this far more important question: *"Who do you want to be when you grow up?"*

Who you eventually become as a woman can either be an accident or part of what you decide about yourself right now. For example, do you want to be a failure, a criminal who ends up in prison, a drug addict, a homeless person or a drunk, in later life? Probably not. But it's amazing how many men and women turn out that way. In some tragic cases, they become all of those things.

One thing's for sure, it wasn't part of their plan. Or maybe they simply didn't have a plan at all. Perhaps they were 'too busy' at the time. Are you too busy to decide who you want to be? Or perhaps it seems too much effort? How people end up in bad situations can be incredibly complicated. Bad luck certainly plays a part, but, in its simplest form, how our lives turn out is about the sequence of small, seemingly unimportant decisions we all make (or avoid making) every day of our lives.

As a child, all our decisions tend to be made by our parents or carers. By the time you become a teenager, you're probably sick and tired of this. But because so many young people in 'civilised' societies aren't allowed to make decisions for many years, when you finally have to, you don't always know how to do it. It's only when you start having to make most of your own decisions that you begin to realise having others make them all for you is actually a lot easier. A major part of becoming a woman is about how you make large and small decisions, and fully accepting the consequences of your decisions without blaming anyone else.

sweet experiment
In the 1960s, a group of young children became part of an experiment by the psychologist Walter Mischel at Stanford University in the USA. These four-year-olds were given a simple choice: they could have one or two marshmallows. They could have one immediately. Or if they were prepared to wait twenty minutes, they would be given two marshmallows. It was a small decision. Or was it? About fourteen years later, these same children were tracked down. The researchers made an amazing discovery. The kids who were able to wait for twenty minutes were happier, more successful and effective at school, and more confident socially.

An ability in their early years to make the decision to delay gratification by controlling their impulsiveness made a huge difference in later years. Do you think people who end up in jail or as addicts would have been one or two marshmallows kids? My guess is they would say, *"Give me one and **now**!!"*

Knowing how important it is to your longer-term happiness and success to be able to control your impulsiveness will have a significant effect on what sort of woman you turn out to be.

One of the biggest problems in our consumer society is that we are all bombarded hour after hour, year after year by messages trying to persuade us to buy all sorts of stuff that promises to make us happy, fulfilled, to look cool, sexy, etc. The marketing of many products is designed specifically to make us more impulsive. We are brainwashed into believing we can have everything now. And we are told all sorts of rubbish to persuade us to not delay our gratification. We'll take a closer look at how to make better decisions in a later chapter.

> *"As a younger woman you believe that if you don't do certain things (like getting married or having children) by a certain time your chances of fulfilment will be gone. This is **not true**. Focus on growing, learning, developing, travelling, experiencing, having fun and enjoying good friends. The more you do that, the more a person you become, the more you will be loved, respected and noticed by the right people."* Katrien Van der Veere

> *"Being a woman is about learning to believe in yourself. And knowing who you are."*
> Chrissie Godson

Ashley Schwartau of ManagedMischief.com summed up the difference between being a girl and a woman when she told me, *"None of the OMGs will matter in ten years!"*

what I wish I'd known about:

looking after myself

During the week we often treat our bodies like temples. But at the weekends they become amusement parks.

Pause and think before you answer the following question: how well do you really look after yourself? This chapter covers a number of loosely related topics. In isolation, some may not appear that important. However, it's the combined effect of what you'll read that determines how well you are looking after yourself. The habits you develop when you are young will have a profound effect on your future health and well-being.

Perhaps you think you look after yourself pretty well right now, but let's start by asking you how often you allow your inner voice to talk to you in a tone you would never tolerate from your worst enemy? Do you tell yourself off all the time? *"I look fat!" "I'm so hairy!" "Why am I so stupid, stupid, stupid?"* (We'll discuss in more detail in a later chapter how this constant internal conversation cripples millions of young women.)

the basics

How often do you deliberately deprive yourself of normal levels of sleep? A distraught mother once asked me to talk to her 'impossible' teenage daughter. This girl was particularly rude, irritable and moody. She regularly had tantrums and screaming fits, making life a misery for her entire family. Grudgingly she agreed to talk to me about her 'problem'. She didn't look at me. With her arms folded, she slowly opened up and told me how she felt most of the time. She was utterly exhausted. The bags under her eyes confirmed that she wasn't getting anything like enough sleep. But why? Too much partying perhaps? No. Not at all.

She loved reading, especially in bed. She would force herself to stay awake to read. Then when she finally put her books down, she couldn't sleep. Her brain became so overactive she couldn't relax. It was as if she'd managed to confuse her body so much that her brain no longer knew whether her bed was the place for her to sleep or to stay awake. We came up with a simple solution. Her parents immediately bought her a comfy chair for her room. She could read as much as she wanted to, but only in the chair, not in her bed. This was an essential part of re-educating her brain to know that when she got into bed, it was to sleep. She agreed. The results were astonishing. And immediate. Within the first week, she was getting an extra three hours sleep every night; that's tweny-one hours extra sleep per week, which is the equivalent of three additional nights of sleep every week. Her behaviour towards her family was totally transformed too. All because she was now getting enough sleep. Simple.

Next question: how much water do you drink every day? Most men and women of all ages don't drink enough water. Our bodies need water. We forget. Try this experiment; identify people you know who drink a lot of water, perhaps instead of other beverages such as tea, coffee or alcohol. They probably have far more energy than most people, their skin is clearer and their weight is under control. Water nourishes the body, and flushes unwanted toxins out of our bodies. For proof, water a dry plant, and watch how within an hour its leaves will pick up and flourish. Your mind and body reacts the same way. Drink more water.

Human beings are designed to move. Countless older women consistently tell me their biggest regret is not making it a priority throughout their life to stay physically fit. They fooled themselves into believing they didn't have the time. Think of physical activity as 'play', not 'work.' Many people are put off by exercise because it's called a 'workout'.

One woman I spoke to in her eighties suffers from chronic leg pain. She told me she 'knows' that she's paying the price today for never looking after her body. Does this mean obsessive gym and/or fitness classes for you? Not at all. In fact, too much exercise can be harmful, if it becomes yet another obsession. For some it becomes a way of punishing themself for (or justifying) over-eating.

A brisk twenty minute walk every day is a great start to any day. Walking is the best way to lose excess weight. It doesn't require any expensive equipment or memberships. It's 'low-impact' which means you are least likely to hurt yourself. And it burns more fat than just about any other form of physical activity. Perhaps with the exception of swimming. Walking also clears the mind and fosters a feeling of well-being.

Sally Helvey is in her early fifties. *"I discovered yoga later in life. It is the best stress-buster. And helps open up my mind and body to better cope with emotional or physical problems. I wish I'd found yoga years ago."* Similarly, millions of busy women are huge fans of Pilates.

Yoga and Pilates are a fantastic way to calm the mind, but a bigger benefit is how these forms of exercise gently stretch all your muscles (including the heart) to improve blood flow, body flexibility and inner strength. Regular muscle stretching will naturally improve and enhance your feminine body shape.

We all have enough time for what is important enough to us. Find an enjoyable form of physical exercise and make it part of your future life – today.

Now how about the food and drink you consume? And how much (or how little)? Which of the following best describes you? Are you:

1) An under-eater?
2) An over-eater?
3) A 'yo-yo' eater? Or
4) A normal eater?

An under-eater is anyone who deliberately starves herself by consuming fewer nutrients than her body needs in order to function at peak health. She may believe she's too fat, even when she isn't. An over-eater obviously consumes more food than she needs. The excess food then gets stored as unwanted fat. A 'yo-yo' eater is someone who under-eats for a while, gives in to their will-power and then over-eats by binging, then feels really bad about what they believe is their weakness and for 'failing' (yet again) at their latest diet.

Perversely, normal eaters have become the rarest type of woman in developed countries around the world. We'll explore what normal eating is, and how to become one, in a moment.

Those who under, over, or yo-yo eat, have their own personal reasons for their disorders (and these are disorders). Let's look at some of the most common reasons why unhealthy and (even fatal) eating disorders amongst young women have reached such epidemic proportions.

"Before I was a model I had a healthy self-esteem. That began to change. It was a 'normal' day being looked at, and openly discussed, often quite disdainfully and dismissively by advertising art directors and other creatives. I was naturally skinny (I never dieted, ever) but they'd say ,"She's too fat, too boney, too androgynous, too 'whatever'". Rejection is such a daily part of life for a professional model. You think you deal with it. But, especially when you're young, you don't. Obviously it hurts. You think it's normal but it's not.

"Today, far too many young women choose to reject themselves. It's so sad. Anything you repeatedly tell yourself that's self-critical can take you to a dangerous place. I'm convinced that 'body dysmorphia', when you don't see the reality of what's in the mirror, has become a self-inflicted disease among so many women because of our obsessive focus on what we think is 'wrong' about our bodies. Anorexic women see themselves as 'fat' of course, but almost every woman thinks their body has faults. But no one else sees them. It's true that the last time most of us felt great about our bodies was when we were three or four years of age!" Kate Sturgess, former model

Lyndsay Russell is the author of the satirical novel *Making it Big* (www.MakingItBigTheBook.com) which describes a world in which being 'big' is something women aspire to, rather than being size zero.

"My girlfriend is a top digital retoucher. I know through her work how many images we see around us every day have been 'stretched' to give someone who's already a strikingly slim model an extra long waist/legs etc. It's far more extensive than we realise and totally impossible to live up to. This kind of retouching now happens even in mundane catalogues. It's quite shocking. These images are not showing how 99.9% of women actually look! And the 0.1% who might look that way, are more than likely dissatisfied with some part of their body anyway, striving to look like a retouched image they've seen of a rival model!

"When I was in my teens and twenties, I thought I looked fat and was never happy with

my body. I look back on those photos now and can't believe why I ever thought I looked bad. We are doing a lot of the mental damage to ourselves."

So, for a moment, think of your body and your skin as the most precious, must-have, designer handbag. It is truly remarkable. It has been handcrafted specifically for you. There is only one of its kind. This handbag holds everything about you together in one place: all of your organs, muscles, blood and bones. And all of your emotions and thoughts, some of which are lighter than air, helping you float more easily through life, while others can weigh you down, making you feel sluggish, depressed and disheartened. In some cases, we feel so bad about ourselves, we consciously or subconsciously punish that handbag. Even though it might be doing the best it can, working for an impossibly difficult boss – you.

And remember, it's the only one you've got. Every day for your entire life you will be putting things into that handbag. Imagine, the supple skin of this gorgeous tote has the ability to stretch to bursting when it's overfilled, to shrink to its perfect size (or even shrivel up to a size that's smaller than it should be). Treasure it as something special. Nourish it. Be more aware what you put inside. Don't use it as a place to dump stuff. It will ruin how you feel about it. Keep it pristine, polish it, and show it off. There are large bags and small bags and every size in between. This is your bag, regardless of the size. Be proud and take great care of it.

how to be a 'normal eater'

Normal eaters don't diet. If you'd prefer to be a normal eater, dump the very idea of a diet today. Never go on another restrictive diet ever again. Science and detailed research has proved categorically that diets do not work anyway. You are statistically more likely to put back on (with interest) any weight you lose on a short-term deprivation-based diet.

Obesity is the biggest health problem in America today. And that's where they have the largest diet industry. The multi-billion dollar global diet industry is making millions of women fat. And causing untold pain and suffering among those who would prefer to be slim but have yet to figure out how to lose their excess weight and keep it off. Every time a diet fails, as they usually do, we blame ourselves, not the people who are making their absurd promises.

Before we explore a successful, permanent alternative to dieting, consider this idea from Eastern philosophy: everyone has inside himself or herself a 'hungry ghost'. This hungry ghost has a constant craving and a number of appetites that are difficult or even impossible to satisfy. This includes emotional ones too. It has a huge belly, and a massive mouth but a very slim, narrow throat. No matter how much we put into that big mouth, the narrow throat stops most of it reaching the stomach; so the hungry ghost always stays hungry. Worse still, the hungry ghost has put your taste buds in charge.

No matter how much we put into our mouths in an attempt to satisfy these appetites it never does. We go through life constantly feeling hungry, trying to satisfy what will never be satisfied. How active is your hungry ghost?

Each time you open the refrigerator or pick up something in a shop or cafe that's made to look like it's a 'food', stop and ask yourself whether you are really hungry or is this yet another insatiable craving by your hungry ghost? Better still, anytime you think you feel hungry, drink some water instead. In so many cases, your body isn't hungry, it's actually thirsty.

Trying to satisfy these different types of hunger is so often for emotional nourishment, rather than to feed and strengthen our bodies. Everyone wants to feel 'good' about themselves. When we feel 'bad', for a whole range of trivial or serious reasons, we so often feed the hungry ghost with unhealthy foods. When we eat rubbish, our stomachs become a bit like those massive garbage tips where desperately poor scavengers pick their way through the waste trying to find anything of value they can use to nourish the body. Everything they can't use immediately they save in a pocket or sack. Your body is the same, and what it cannot use immediately goes into storage as unwanted fat. Because your internal scavengers haven't been able to extract enough nutrition from the rubbish you may have eaten, they send requests to the brain to keep eating until they've found enough nutrition. That's where cravings come from. By improving what you eat, those internal scavengers find everything they need from a much smaller pile of food. And they don't have to put any of it into storage.

Furthermore, because we know subconsciously that we're eating unhealthy food, we often eat quickly, to minimise the 'crime'. When we've finished the entire packet in record time (these foods are almost always in a packet) we then feel full, bloated and guilty (again). Realise that this 'fake' food has been manufactured in order to make large corporations fat. Making you fat, too, is merely a side effect for them. So long as you keep coming back for more they are very happy indeed.

But for you, self-loathing sometimes follows and the cycle starts all over again. It's time for more of that yo-yo eating.

It's also worth mentioning that the food industry has brainwashed millions of people into believing that 'fat' is the enemy. It's not. You actually need some fat in your diet.

The silent, cheap and deadly enemy is actually

sugar. Sugar is ladled in vast quantities into almost every processed food. Foods labelled as 'low fat' are routinely very high in sugar. Avoid any food that includes in its list of ingredients anything your grandmother, or great grandmother would not have had in their store cupboard. Actively cut down on your sugar intake. And that includes alcohol.

alcohol

Alcohol is highly calorific, which is reason enough to consume it moderately. But of course alcohol isn't like other foods, is it? No book is ever going to stop people drinking if they want to (full disclosure: I enjoy beer and wine myself). Alcohol is marketed as a stimulant. It's not. It's actually a depressant. You only see happy, 'beautiful people' drinking in commercials. Images of depressed, hopelessly drunken women, throwing up in the gutter late at night, going home with a guy they don't know or wouldn't be seen dead with while sober, don't seem to feature much for some reason. Nor does the 'walk of shame' the next morning...

Just be aware that if you ever find yourself 'needing' a few drinks to relax, or to feel more confident, it is a quiet alarm bell of a possible future drink problem. As a general rule, have at least three days every week free of any alcohol consumption. It gives your liver some time to metabolise the alcohol and return to a normal state. And it shows you don't yet have an alcohol dependency. Be aware, too, that addiction is a disease that runs in the family, and you may be more prone than your friends.

the habits of slim people

Naturally slim people have different habits that keep them slim. Doesn't it make more sense to copy what they do instead of going through life starving yourself, binging, starving, binging, etc?

What follows is a brief summary of *The Seven Secrets of Slim People*, a great book by Vicki Hansen and Shane Goodman. The book includes some very helpful worksheets. It's my belief that if the contents of their book were taught to millions of young children, obesity and the huge increases in diabetes and heart disease could be reduced quite radically around the world. These are some of their key recommendations.

The authors claim that your weight is not the problem. Excess weight is the symptom of the problem. They believe that self-imposed deprivation and trying to control your intake of food leads to over-eating. They say *"Trust your body, and not your mind."* Because your body knows more about what it needs than you do.

Millions of women have developed an obsession about not eating, which consumes their lives. And feel their weight is completely out of control. If you try to control what you eat, the food will always win. Get out of your own way and let your body decide what you need to eat.

A diet is a self-imposed famine. Every time your body goes into famine mode, it slows down to conserve as much energy as possible. This is designed to protect you. Dieting slows down your metabolic rate from anything between 15% and 40%. And can take up to a year to return to normal. However, when you end your self-imposed famine, you again consume more calories, but your metabolism stays low. Therefore you get fat. Again. Your body stores that fat in anticipation of the next time you decide to have a personal famine.

To become a normal eater you must unlearn the unhealthy relationship you may have created around food, and the perception you have about your weight. You can trust yourself and your body. Listen to it more closely and accept it for what it is (don't listen to the hungry ghost). Also, accept your feelings, but break the link you've created between your emotions and food.

The subconscious link between your self-image and food has a real impact on your body and on your emotions. Do you think of yourself as a fat person? If so, you are focused on an image of yourself, not the real you. But if that is how you define yourself, your body will act as if it is supposed to be fat (and your hungry ghost will happily cooperate). This starts a cycle of hating your body more, treating it with disrespect, disgust or shame. Making things worse. So think of yourself as just you, and that you can be a slim person (especially if you're not slim just yet). Your body will actually regulate to the size of a slim person, if you let it. If you've convinced yourself that you will be more attractive or more lovable if you're slimmer, you have decided subconsciously that you're unlovable at the moment. And that's not true: you are lovable right now, regardless of your size.

You really can learn simple and sensible eating habits that do not require you to ever deprive yourself and, more importantly, deprive your body of what it needs to take you through life in full health. Hansen and Goodman claim that our widespread obsession with food is a form of eating disorder in itself. Paradoxically, the only time we don't think of food is when we are actually eating it. We eat on the run, too busy doing other things to give what we consume any meaningful thought or appreciation in those crucial moments. Young women have been tricked and brainwashed into believing that skinny is beautiful. Looking malnourished is only a small step from being malnourished.

- From today, refuse to compare yourself with the size and shape of any other woman.
- Listen to your body. Learn what your body actually needs, not what it craves.
- Stop letting your decisions about food and what

you eat get in the way of the job your body already knows how to do.

- Stop weighing out your food, or 'counting calories'.
- From now on, never eat 'on the run' or while you're doing something else. Sit down to eat. Concentrate totally on what you are eating. Give it your full attention.
- Eat s-l-o-w-l-y. This is an absolutely essential element of normal eating.
- Eat only when you are physically hungry. Ignore set 'meal times'.
- Don't eat 'now', so you're not hungry 'later'.
- Understand the 0-10 hunger scale; 0 is when you are not at all hungry. In fact, you are so stuffed with food, one more mouthful, you'll think you might explode. 4-5 you're getting hungry but 6-7 is the time to eat. 8-10 you will be so hungry you run the very real risk of over-eating.
- Listen to what your body needs to nourish itself. Eat what you want most.
- Only eat the equivalent of your scrunched up fist at any one time. It might not seem like much. But it's about the size your stomach is supposed to be.
- If necessary, put your fork down in between mouthfuls.
- Chew properly.
- Stop eating when you are satisfied, not when you're full.
- Leave food on your plate. It tells your brain that there is no scarcity of food. Do this if you were brought up to believe that there are starving kids in Africa and you have a duty to eat for them.
- Notice how your body feels just after you've eaten.

You can decide today to fully enjoy the body you have

for all its gloriousness, or you can carry on squandering your time and energy for decades to come, desperately trying to turn it into something it's not: a different size, shape or even a different colour. You can spend a fortune (cosmetically or even surgically) vainly trying to 'improve' it, or you can decide today to make friends with your body. Really get to know it, to respect it, to appreciate it for what it does for you and realise that you are the perfect size and shape for you.

> *"I wish I had known in my teen years was that I was perfect just the way I was. I had no self-esteem and sought comfort first in food, then approval from everyone but myself. First love yourself and know you are perfect as you are!!"* Sherrie Tennessee, MBA

Reeva Dunning Putney is an eighty-three-year-old mother.

> *"I remember excitedly visiting my gorgeous girlfriend the morning after she had won Miss World. She was staring at her semi-naked body in the mirror, crying. I gave her an enormous hug and asked what on earth was the matter? She replied: 'I hate my body, look at all that hair!' (She had slightly hairy arms). I guess it just goes to show that even the most beautiful woman in the world can think she's not good enough! So very sad. And rather insane of us women, don't you think?"*

> *"I wish I could have known that it is fun to take care of myself and that looking for a husband was not the answer to feeling safe in the world."* Anonymous woman.

what I wish I'd known about:

my emotions

In the same way that certain foods lead inevitably to emissions of unwanted gas, do you find yourself feeding your mind with so many unhelpful thoughts that it's only a matter of time before there's an inevitable and unwanted reaction: namely an 'emotional fart'?

How often have you had recurring unhelpful thoughts that ferment and stew inside, until one day they can't be contained any longer? You might have lost your temper over something seemingly insignificant. Perhaps you spoke harshly and later wished you could 'un-say' whatever you blurted out. But you can't.

Genuinely happy, calm and relaxed people don't suffer from these 'emotional farts'. They don't sulk, scream, shout or have tantrums. They're not 'difficult' or demanding. They don't whine and complain. Why is that, do you think?

Could it be that their emotional state is in complete harmony with their surroundings? Emotionally stable, they are quietly confident that they can cope with whatever life throws at them. They view life as it is, rather than being obsessed with the way it 'should' be. People with this type of emotional balance are highly appealing to others. And whether or not you feel like this now, you can learn to be like this.

Your body is run on muscle and hormones. And all those hormones flowing through your brain mean your emotions seem to change by the hour, or even by the minute, seemingly for no reason at all. It's no exaggeration to say that a deeper understanding of how you feel, and a recognition of the various emotional states you can fall into, are key to your future happiness.

They will help you foster beneficial emotional states and identify the early warnings of the unhelpful ones, allowing you to head them off. All of this will have a significant impact on how you interact with others.

Daniel Goleman in his groundbreaking book *Emotional Intelligence* wrote, *"People with well-developed emotional skills are also more likely to be content and effective in their lives, mastering the habits of mind that foster their own productivity; people who cannot marshal some control over their emotional life fight inner battles that sabotage their ability for focused work and clear thought."*

How do you adopt and absorb these emotional skills? Becoming more self-aware is the first step. Recognising the triggers that set you off is a valuable, long-lasting life skill. Learning how to manage the broad range of your emotions is what this chapter is all about.

your emotional core

Our Physical Core is the collection of deep muscles in and around the trunk and pelvis. This Core provides inner physical strength, flexibility and stability, protecting us from injury. Strengthening the Physical Core is a key objective in Pilates and yoga.

Much the same way as your Physical Core protects and strengthens you physically, a strong Emotional Core protects your inner emotional strength. Emotions can be so uplifting, yet the same power and intensity can cause untold pain and anguish, attacking our hearts and souls like a cancer. The Emotional Core components are:

- Self-Esteem,
- Attitude,
- Happiness, and
- Kindness, combined with Compassion.

When you improve your self-esteem, you feel more at ease with yourself. By accepting yourself, you become less 'needy' of others. Moving from a low self-esteem to a healthy one, also improves self-confidence. When you start exhibiting a natural sense of quiet self-confidence, you become more appealing to those around you. And to yourself.

Once you've improved your attitude towards yourself, this improves the attitude towards those you live and work with. More people will almost certainly respond to you more positively. This in turn contributes to your own sense of well-being. It also reduces stress, making you a calmer and more relaxed individual. This further increases the likelihood that even more people will respond better to you.

Combining an improved attitude towards yourself and others, with an improved self-esteem, increases the likelihood you will start to feel happier in yourself. You can amplify this even further by adopting simple, yet effective happiness strategies, which again strengthen your entire Emotional Core. Each one feeds and nourishes the others. There are a number of steps that you can take right now to improve your Emotional Core. That's what this chapter is about.

Talk to anyone who's had a personal tragedy, and they will tell you their lives changed forever in an instant. Accidents, illnesses and natural phenomena affect countless individuals every single day. Your Emotional Core is the best insurance to cope with the effects of personal traumas. The benefits to you and to those who come into contact with you have the potential to be monumental and long lasting. The more you attract other people, the more you will realise that improvements you have made have had a direct contribution to the way others view you.

explode

Of course, we all have faults and farts. Some minor, while others are far more serious and have a hugely damaging effect. An under-developed Emotional Core can be a trigger, turning minor faults into major ones.

We all have our own ways of coping with stress or being upset. Taking it out on those closest to you isn't going to make you more appealing to them. Or to anyone else. Screaming, shouting, and tantrums are common among young children, but take those behaviours into adulthood, and you'll find that it's simply not acceptable.

In violent family environments, it might be seen as 'normal'. It isn't. If you have such experiences, you need to unlearn some of those behaviours in adult life, if you are going to function as a more effective person.

implode

Have you learned to totally contain your emotions? Some people never show them. This isn't healthy either. It's often the case of children in families where parents don't express themselves openly and respectfully. Have you learned to deal with your own emotions by 'imploding'? This is a bit like a cartoon character that swallows a stick of dynamite. The dynamite goes off and the character blows up like a balloon before returning to its original shape. They open their mouth and a small whiff of smoke completes the comedic effect. The only problem with this 'solution' in real life is it never tackles the root cause of the suffering. And each time you get upset for any reason, the latest suffering gets added to your 'collection'.

In his book, *Don't Sweat The Small Stuff*, the late Richard Carlson PhD described unhelpful thoughts as 'snowball thinking'. A small snowball thought gathers more and more unhelpful snow, until it has grown to an enormous size. If you are spending a lot of time on your own, thinking about yourself, your life, what you feel you deserve but are not getting, opportunities missed, regrets and unfulfilled dreams and desires, it is fairly likely a small snowball thought will similarly gather size and importance. But only in your head.

An example of 'snowball thinking' might start along these lines. Someone has said or done something that you don't understand. Nothing 'bad' as such, but a bit confusing. So you start thinking about it. In fact, you try to analyse it, over and over again. This tiny snowball is starting to gain in size. Because you have now devoted so much time thinking about it, you have finally figured out what it 'really' meant. What was originally a theory has now been allowed to become a significant issue. Now you have convinced yourself that you 'know' what it meant. And it wasn't good. In fact, it is now proof that yet again someone has disrespected you. Or they have failed to live up to your expectations. *"How could they?"* *"What a bastard/bitch!"*

The other person is totally unaware of any wrongdoing. Why? Because there was no wrong-doing. But how do you think they'd get treated the next time they got together? A massive 'Emotional Fart'!

Have you ever had any such experiences yourself? Either as a victim or as the perpetrator? We all have.

Here's the critical point: the above reaction had nothing to do with the person's original behaviour. It was entirely down to the fact that 'snowball thinking' attached a series of incorrect meanings and assumptions to that innocent behaviour. This is the problem with overanalysis. As each wrong assumption is added into the mix, its destructive power grows.

What needs to be recognised is how and why those assumptions came about in the first place.

Our past relationship experiences create our life story. Unfortunately, in so many cases the story we tell ourselves is different from reality. When we combine all the wrong assumptions, judgements, interpretations, distortions and filters we end up with a mishmash of half-truths, confusion, suffering and insecurities. Most of which we are not even consciously aware of.

What recurring thoughts do you have that are not helping you lead a happier life? Imagine your life if you didn't spend so much time exhausting yourself by giving these unhelpful thoughts more attention than they deserve.

A well-developed Emotional Core protects you. It provides you with more emotional stability, flexibility and inner strength. When you know deep down you have a stronger Emotional Core, those resources help you cope with everything life throws at you.

what you need to know about:

self-esteem

Self-esteem is the first of the four Emotional Core components. Let's explore what self-esteem is, how your past and current thinking patterns and behaviour influence your self-confidence. First the good news: weak, needy and inadequate 'victims' with little or no self-confidence and low self-esteem are in high demand these days.

Now the bad news: controlling bullies just love them. And the more insecure and unloved anyone feels about themselves, the easier it is for the unscrupulous to entice them into a life of unrewarding servitude, keeping them under their control by dishing out daily doses of cruel put-downs, psychological and emotional, as well as physical abuse. And each time they get away with it, it confirms in the mind of the victim that they 'deserve' such harsh treatment because they really are that inadequate. In many cases, those with chronically poor self-confidence sentence themselves to years of emotional torment and abuse because they are willing to settle for anyone who shows interest in them.

"*I didn't set out to be a model: I was a real tomboy and rarely wore make-up, nail polish or read women's magazines, though as it turned out, I was often in them!*

"*I was puzzled when I used to go to parties, to find that absolutely nobody talked to me. I genuinely thought no one liked me. It took me quite a while to realise that because of my looks, men were too scared of me. And women mistrusted me because they saw me as a threat. I lived the dream of millions of young women. Yet it was like I was a freak of nature. It was weird.*

"*As beautiful as I was paid to be, it didn't stop my own low self-esteem harming my relationships; I had a habit of singling out the most unsuitable guys. I was brilliant at pressing the self-destruct button. Every time a relationship went wrong, I'd then be able to blame myself because I 'knew' it would turn out that way. I was always attracted to men who said they 'needed' me rather than 'wanted' me. I came to realise that if you believed you deserved to be treated badly, you attracted that.*

"*If young women could learn how to invest more energy enhancing their self-esteem rather than their outer appearance, there'd be millions of happier women in the world.*" Kate Sturgess, former model.

On a scale of 0–10, how high is your self-esteem and self-confidence right now?

Extremely low self-esteem can mean you feel deeply unhappy and sense that you get walked over all the time, but you're not quite sure why. So less than a 5 is a sign that you would benefit from giving your self-esteem some much needed attention.

Anything above a 5 is fairly healthy, although there's probably room for improvement. Is it possible to have self-esteem and self-confidence that's too high? Yes. Extreme selfishness or believing that the world revolves around you can make you deeply unappealing to others.

Aim for 'Goldilocks' self-esteem: not too much, not too little, juuuuust right. Without a healthy self-esteem, emotional instability is practically guaranteed. That applies whether your self-esteem is too high, or too low.

reservoir of suffering

Each time someone calls us hurtful names, especially people who claim to love us (and that includes ourselves), the remarks flow into what I call our Reservoir of Suffering. At the bottom of this reservoir is our self-esteem. It just sits there minding its own business. But as each new 'hurt' gets poured on top, that self-esteem is crushed by the sheer weight and pressure bearing down on it. Much like a shipwreck at the bottom of the ocean, our self-esteem is confined to the depths of our despair. Our self-esteem is drowned by the combined effect of these slurs and put-downs.

Low self-esteem directly affects the relationship you have with yourself as well as your relationships with others, your physical and mental health and your attitudes towards sex: turning some people off sex entirely or leading to a sex addiction in others. It can also lead to eating disorders as well as drug or alcohol abuse. Increased stress induces irritability, headaches and stomach aches, accompanied by a recurring sense of feeling overwhelmed. Low self-esteem can lead to a combination of other debilitating emotions and behaviours that make life even more miserable. But it can be improved if you decide to make it a personal priority. Let's see how, because the benefits can be life-transforming.

Commercial divers lift precious artefacts from the depths of the sea by attaching buoyancy aids to help with the lifting. So it is with salvaging your own self-esteem, one of the most precious cargos you possess. It can take a while, and requires some effort on your part. Especially when you consider how many forces are at work to push it down again.

Propaganda experts know that the lies and distortions they spread become 'facts' if they get repeated enough. But you can make this same process work for the good, too. Repetition is the key to improving your self-esteem. This is why making daily affirmations can be so effective. The more time you choose to invest in improving your self-esteem, the quicker and easier it will be to make and see long-term improvements. You really can do it.

Help from friends will add even more oxygen to fuel your recovery and inflate those buoyancy bags to lift your self-esteem back to the surface. So, make a decision to adopt small improvements every day.

Asking for help is often thought of as a sign of weakness: proof that we are indeed as pathetic as we have been told. We have too many problems, not enough time, or not enough money to do this 'right now'. These are excuses, not reasons. Asking for help is not a weakness, it can be a valuable solution.

your inner critic

Sadly, after years of being put down, or being made to

feel bad about yourself, we learn to put ourselves down before anyone else can 'get in first'. By doing this, we are fooled into believing we have insulated ourselves from being hurt by others, but it's the equivalent of punching ourselves in the face. Nip this in the bud by recognising when you do, then stop it.

Often we've faced years of insults and put-downs from a parent or so-called friends who, despite this, profess to love and care about you. If that's the case, whatever they say must be true, right? Wrong. However, our inner critic often agrees with these put-downs. Even though the basis for the put-downs is false, we often believe them.

We all have an 'inner voice'. This voice can be supportive or destructive. The inner voice of those with low self-esteem tends to become their most savage and vicious critic.

If you're thinking right now, *"I don't have an inner voice."* That was it.

Our inner voice can be encouraging, helpful and supportive. Think of this voice as a potential coach. If you were an international athlete, how well do you think you would perform if you were constantly told how incapable you were of winning any races, or improving on your previous 'personal best'? Who would want a coach like that? But it's surprising how many of us allow our inner voice to drag us down. Its motives are sometimes honourable. Unfortunately, it doesn't always do a great job. It can get a lot of things wrong about you.

For example, if your inner voice thinks you won't be able to achieve something, it may be negative in order to protect you from feeling so bad when (not if) you fail. The voice knows that if you don't try something, you cannot possibly succeed. Therefore, you don't try, you therefore fail to succeed and the voice proves that it was correct.

Whatever you do to rebuild your self-esteem, much of that effort will be wasted if you don't redefine the relationship you have with that inner voice. No matter what progress you make in other areas of your life, if your inner voice is highly critical, it will scupper most of your efforts, dragging your self-esteem back down to the bottom of your Reservoir of Suffering.

That voice has been with you for so long, you have probably never questioned the accuracy of anything it has said to you, or its motives. Your inner voice can be your own personal ambassador, but often it's an assassin.

What scripts has your inner voice used against you, perhaps for years? Does it tell you what you aren't capable of? Why you don't deserve to be happy? How and why you are unworthy of anything better?

how to take back control

How might you behave differently if your critic was not trying so hard to control you? Remember this voice is not you. It's someone who wants to control you. Give your inner critic a name. It doesn't have to be a flattering one. You can disagree with this voice. You can argue with it. Although it's probably not a good idea to do this aloud unless you know you are alone. Confront your critic. Prove your critic wrong. Ask or even tell your critic to shut up. When you hear negative comments from your critic, yell at it *"Delete, delete, delete."* or *"Shut up and get lost."* *"You're poison. Go away."* Come up with your own comments if these aren't strong enough for you.

What if you could turn down the volume of your inner critic, or even switch it off? Actually, you own it, and can do with it whatever you want. Do what you want, not what it wants.

Let's suppose you have learned to believe you are stupid. You can prove such an idea is totally incorrect.

Let's do it. For the purposes of this exercise, make a list of situations or incidents where you have behaved in a way that demonstrates conclusively that you are not stupid. What good decisions have you made? What good results have you created? What are your best achievements? At first, you may find it difficult to come up with examples, but despite negative comments from others and your inner critic, you have achieved a great deal in life already.

Universal put-downs that go unchallenged contribute to at least a dampening of an otherwise healthy self-esteem. When you hear your inner critic using words such as *"always"*, *"never"*, *"you should"*, *"you must"* – challenge it; demand proof that what it says is true. When you become more self-aware, you may discover these words are used far too much. In fact, remove the words *"should"* and *"must"* from your own vocabulary. These are 'loaded' words and easily lead to feelings of shame, guilt and disapproval. Become more aware of others who accuse you of *"You always..."* and *"You never..."*. They are trying to exert power over you. Don't let them. Increased awareness will help you question the motives of those around you. In the same way critics have repeatedly put you down over the years, it's essential you learn a new habit of repeating healthy thoughts.

Never ever put yourself down on a date, or draw attention to what you think are your shortcomings. If you really can't resist saying things like *"I feel fat in this"* save it for your closest girlfriends. Never to boyfriends or work colleagues. It's off-putting. Reverse the situation: would you think a man sexy, or a boss in control, who says *"My nose looks so big"*, or *"I hate my flabby belly"*?

Notice more of your successes. Every time you do something right, quietly congratulate yourself. You're slowly starting to prove your inner critic wrong, and clearing space in your mind for a constructive coach to contribute to your long-term well-being. This will help you become even more appealing to others.

sometimes it's not about the inner voice

Your self-esteem isn't only eroded by the inner voice. Sometimes it is your emotional make-up itself that does the job. Many women do not distinguish between their emotions and themselves. "*I am my emotions,*" they say, and truly believe it. Which leads to confusion when they experience many different emotions in a short period of time, or even simultaneously. Even without the inner voice, it is easy to think you must be weird, strange or even deranged at these times.

You are not. Everyone is a mass of conflicting emotions, but just like the inner voice, those emotions are not *you*, they are merely part of the totality that is you. Emotions are part of the complexity of being human. You can learn to control and channel them in positive directions which will help boost your self-esteem.

practical ways to boost self-esteem

When you improve your self-esteem, you increase your options. You feel better about doing so, which in turn takes your self-esteem up a notch.

From now on, make a decision not to allow your inner critic to say anything that undermines you. Ever. And stop letting your inner critic blame you for anything. It's probably wrong about you – yet again. It may take some time to retrain yourself and silence your inner critic, but you can do it.

If others tend to put you down, decide to be more assertive with them, too. Being assertive is about respecting yourself as much as respecting others. Aggressive behaviour is not to be confused with assertiveness. Aggressiveness is the equivalent of marching into somebody else's country. Assertiveness is standing your ground to ensure nobody marches into yours.

Learn to say *"no"* more often. Wean yourself off saying *"yes"* when you'd prefer to say *"no"*. The fear of disapproval often stops us. In reality, most people tend to think better of those with clear boundaries and who will not allow themselves to be taken advantage of. Someone who expects you always to say *"yes"* may be unhappy when you say *"no"*, but over the long term you may earn more of their respect.

If someone puts you down, or makes jokes at your expense, politely say, *"Please stop doing that. I don't like it."* If they dismiss your request, repeat what you said calmly and politely. Or you could respond by saying something like, *"Some need to put down others to feel better about themselves. I hope you're feeling a bit better now. Pick on someone else next time."* If they insist on making fun of you for being *"so sensitive"*, respond by saying that perhaps they are the one who's being insensitive. Or simply leave the room if you can. Just because you allowed this treatment in the past, it doesn't mean it should be allowed to continue. It is better that they think you have no sense of humour than to allow them to make you feel bad about yourself. Just stop everybody from getting away with it. Do it calmly. There is no need to get irate or emotional. But learn to do it.

In general, stop letting others have what they want at your expense. Each time you allow this to happen, it chips away a little more of your self-esteem and reinforces any feelings of inferiority you might have. Stop making assumptions about what people think of you. You cannot read their minds, so don't be so sure they think poorly of you.

Identify the toxic people in your life: those who

make you feel bad, deflated or worn out. Make a decision to minimise the time spent with them. If you can't avoid at least some contact, make a concerted effort not to tell them about your plans and aspirations so they won't try to talk you out of pursuing what you want.

Instead, invest more time with the people that make you feel good about yourself.

Who do you perceive as the authority figures in your life? Inevitably, parents are on the list. Gaining approval from these authority figures is usually important for most people, but there are some who are cruel and not supportive. If some of your authority figures have practically made a career out of putting you down, perhaps it's time to delete them from your list of people from whom you seek approval. After all, they've never done it before, so it's unlikely they ever will.

List everything you like about yourself. Ask your friends what they think you're particularly good at. Ask only those you trust. Don't include anyone who puts you down.

List your achievements. If it helps, carry a note pad around with you for a while, to write down your past achievements as you think of them.

- What is working in your life?
- What isn't working as well as you might like?
- What actions can you take to improve the areas that aren't working?

Decide to do something new every day. Added together, little things can lead to big improvements. List all the places you want to visit and everything you've always wanted to do. From this constantly evolving list, find something each day to look forward to. Use your list to set yourself a new, personal 'enjoyment' goal every month: that's twelve new goals in a year. To make this happen, plan ahead more. Make appointments with yourself. And don't cancel on yourself. Your needs are at least as important as anyone else's.

Ask yourself a few more questions like these:

- If success at anything was guaranteed, what would I do?
- What new skills could I acquire?
- What new interest could I immerse myself in?

New activities can help you break out of the self-destructive thinking that leads to harmful introspection. Worry and guilt have been described as the 'pointless emotions'.

Extremely high-performing individuals in the world are invariably incredibly busy, yet they look after their physical well-being by investing time in themselves for exercise and relaxation. You can do the same, but only after you decide to make 'you' a priority.

Invest time in making friends with yourself first. Even though you may not feel like it, find ways to interact with other people. Exercising at a gym can achieve this.

When someone gives you a compliment, have the grace to accept it. From now on, never invalidate a compliment by dismissing what they have said. It is disrespectful of the giver of the compliment. Simply say, *"Thank you. That was a nice thing to say. I appreciate it."* Never say, *"Oh, it was nothing."* What you have done is not 'nothing'. Be more aware of what you allow into your head.

Accept that you can change if you want to do so enough. All change can be uncomfortable or even frightening at first. Acting 'as if' you have confidence in whatever you do can be a major contributor towards actually being more confident.

By making small changes and improvements, as your confidence grows you become more inclined to make even more changes and improvements. Slowly you will start to notice a change for the better in the way you feel about yourself.

Sometimes we can't seem to help what we think about. Especially if or when we are in emotional pain. You can change your emotions. All it requires is making a choice. You can decide to feel something more empowering and more useful to you.

To illustrate this, do the following exercise. Sit or stand. Look down at the floor; make your shoulders rounded and take on the appearance of a depressed person. Now, without changing your physical posture, try to feel happy. You will probably find this difficult to achieve. Next, stand up straight; look up; breathe deeply. Then, again without changing your posture, try to feel depressed. It's difficult to do so. One of the simplest and most powerful ways to improve the way we feel is to simply stand up straight.

We become what we think about the most. So, practise visualisation. See yourself being more confident and handling situations better. See those around you with happy smiling faces. Expect to be successful. This will improve the likelihood that you will follow through on your new behaviours. Experience feelings of quiet confidence and happiness. Practise your new behaviour with people who don't know you yet.

By adopting these behaviours, you can only become a more attractive person: to yourself, to those you know already and to everyone you have yet to meet. Attractiveness is not the same as being beautiful or handsome. Those are genetic qualities. Attractiveness is an attitudinal quality that arises from healthy self-esteem and an appealing attitude to life. Everyone can be an attractive person.

Learn to accept that it is OK just to be you. Become the person you are meant to be.

what you need to know about:

attitude

Attitude is the second pillar of your Emotional Core. Spotting a bad attitude is so easy, isn't it? Although it's far more difficult to recognise a bad one if it's your own.

All too often a lack of self-confidence and low self-esteem will manifest itself in a poor or unhealthy attitude. This in turn will often create more feelings of low self-esteem and even less self-confidence, leading to a worse attitude. It's a circle of thinking, believing and behaviour that can ultimately poison you.

Your attitude is one of the first things other people always notice about you. A can-do attitude is your most valuable asset. It's free. And it's worth looking after. It's been said that thought, attitude, behaviour and result is an ever-increasing circle or outward spiral of impact. By improving what you think, you change your beliefs. Change your beliefs and you change your behaviour. Change your behaviour and you change the results in your life.

The price of a bad or unhealthy attitude can be huge. Not only to everyone else who comes into contact with you, but to you personally. When you allow your attitude to control you, rather than you controlling it, you become someone who is constantly reacting to your own emotions and moods. In extreme cases, people will avoid you.

For many, it has taken years of diligent effort to achieve world-class status as a negative thinker. If you can identify with this, cleansing yourself of negative thoughts is likely to take a while.

This next exercise will almost certainly offer you invaluable insights. Take your time interviewing yourself (or do it with a trusted friend) using these questions and add any others you can come up with:

- What is your attitude right now? Why?
- How much does your attitude help or hinder you at the moment?
- How much are you a by-product of your moods, or is your mood what you decide it's going to be?
- What do you tend to do or say that might lead others to think that you have an unhealthy attitude at the moment?
- Who affects you positively?
- Who affects you negatively?
- Who do you spend time with who drain you?
- How committed are you to improving your attitude?
- What would you want people to say about you behind your back?
- What do you need to do differently so they would?

Let's be realistic here, very few people are totally positive or totally negative all the time. Who are the people you know who have great attitudes? I'd be prepared to bet that they attract other people like a magnet. They radiate optimism, energy, enthusiasm and vitality. Optimists tend to be happier, more successful and healthier individuals than those with negative attitudes. Spend more time with those optimists. And make sure you are someone they would choose to spend time with too.

Your attitude is linked to your energy level. You can quickly improve your attitude by increasing your energy. Enthusiasm increases energy. So learn to be more enthusiastic. Feeling tired? Ignore those feelings. With some practice, you can nearly always work through them. Focus your attention on what's good about a situation and not what's wrong. Look forward to more things.

People with a great attitude are not 'Me Merchants' or 'I Specialists'. They are people who constantly talk about themselves. Some do so because they are intensely arrogant and self-focused. People who talk incessantly about themselves are far less appealing than those who don't.

Dear Daughter
Avoid unhappy people.

what you need to know about:

happiness

To gain a better understanding of genuine happiness, let's first look at unhappiness.

Happy people are often targeted by very unhappy people who believe they can suck happiness out of those who have it. And when it doesn't work (as it won't), things often get ugly for the victim who then also gets blamed for 'failing' to please.

Knowing more about the various facets of unhappiness, yours and that of others, will give you many insights into how you experience the world. And the effect you have on others. The nature of this topic might seem a bit 'down'; please ignore those feelings. This discussion is designed to help you.

what unhappy people do
I'm reminded of a chat I had with a young guy who claimed he wanted to be in a serious relationship. I started to ask him about happiness. A big mistake. He almost spat, *"I hate all that happy clappy crap."* I

suspect if I'd been a woman he was interested in, he'd have hidden that. Maybe. But it would have come out sometime. Being that unhappy won't help his chances. When someone's default setting is 'unhappy' it will sabotage any present and future relationship.

"*You complete me.*" was a great line from the movie *Jerry Maguire,* but think about the idea behind it just for a moment. If someone else 'completes' you, it actually implies you were imperfect, lacking and incomplete in the first place. When you have a healthy self-esteem and an appealing attitude you are already complete.

Never allow yourself to get sucked into a relationship with an unhappy person. They will want or even insist that they be showered with attention. In almost every case, the giver (you) will fail to give 'enough'.

Therefore, it is essential you learn to identify unhappy people accurately and quickly before you get saddled with the responsibility for 'curing' them. Here are some of the telltale signs:

- Oblivious to the feelings of others, they are only interested in themselves, their own thoughts and feelings.
- They have more rules than they know what to do with. And insist on imposing them on others.
- Constantly finding fault with everyone except themselves, they seek and demand perfection.
- They actively seek conflict to justify releasing suppressed anger or rage.
- They are always 'so busy', either to impress others with their own sense of importance or as a strategy to stop thinking about what isn't working in their life.
- They attempt to control the uncontrollable and demand certainty for everything.
- They feel the world is against them. And things are harder than they need to be. They constantly play the role of a martyr.

- They are chronically fatigued, or want people to think they are, in order to reinforce their martyr status.
- Money is a prime focus, although they often squander it whilst complaining that they never have enough.
- They keep moving the goalposts. Nothing you do for them is right. Even when you do what they tell you, it is never enough.
- If already in a relationship, they aren't interested in the well-being of their partner and don't care about his or her happiness, success, aspirations or comfort. It's always *"me, me, me"*.

Did you read through the list and recognise elements of yourself? Adopting even some of the following ideas will lead to many of these behaviours melting away. You can become happier. One of the ways is to realise that happy people don't make demands on others, nor on themselves. They accept things as they are, and find the courage to take action when improvements are necessary.

assess your current happiness level

1. How much do you want others to be happy? Shrugging your shoulders and not really caring is a good sign that you're not happy yourself.
2. What proportion of your thinking is devoted to what is wrong with your life?
3. What proportion is devoted to what is good or even fantastic about your life?

Does item 2 get more attention than item 3? On a scale of 0–10 how happy would you say you are 'most of the time'?

0 1 2 3 4 5 6 7 8 9 10

Where you place yourself on this scale is what psychologist Martin Seligman of the University of Pennsylvania describes as your 'set-point'. This set-point usually, but not always, remains fairly static through life. Generally speaking, whatever your set-point is today, it will be similar in twenty years time, too. That is, if you carry on with your life as it is today. This is key. Make a permanent change in your attitude towards life and you make a permanent change to your set-point as well.

Anecdotally, I have asked many people of different ages where they would place their happiness level on this scale. The younger people I've asked seem to have an average set-point of 6–7, while older men and women in long-term happy marriages seem to have set-points of 8+. Knowing your happiness set-point can be useful, even if it reminds you that you're basically quite a happy person. If you're set-point is quite low, you can improve it if you decide to make a conscious effort to do so.

Having used these ideas in my own life, my set-point is now about 8 most of the time. Ten years ago it was quite a lot lower, in large part because of my unhelpful thinking patterns. Like everyone else, my set-point fluctuates downwards and upwards on occasion. Ecstasy and joy sometimes visit, too.

For me, I'll experience a 10 simply sitting on the pebbles looking out to sea from Newgale beach in Pembrokeshire, west Wales, near where I grew up. Watching the summer sun go down over St David's Head is only marginally better than sitting in the same place during a raging storm in the middle of winter. It always reconnects me with life. No matter where I am in the world, I've learned to mentally transport myself to that place whenever I'm feeling a bit 'down' or overwhelmed.

You may also have such a place that makes you feel good. Call up such special places in your own mind to help improve your mood when you are down. Visualising like this is a form of 'resourcing', storing pools of positive feelings and retrieving them when you need them.

However, we get so sucked into coping with the day-to-day, we often forget to do what makes us feel happy inside and what is most important to us.

If you are unhappy about elements of your life right now, you are not alone, even though you may often think you are. In recent decades, general levels of happiness in developed countries have dropped noticeably. Unhappiness has therefore become far more widespread. And the number of people suffering from depression has soared. According to the World Health Organization more than 120 million people suffer from depression, which is of course an extreme form of unhappiness.

Depressed people find it particularly difficult to be kind or loving, either to themselves or others.

mindset and match

Genuinely happy people think and behave in fundamentally different ways. There are countless people in dire poverty, enduring appalling living standards and some with horrendous physical handicaps who are far happier than those who appear (on the outside at least) to have everything they could possibly want from life. The way we think is the key.

A dear friend once told me how he often felt disappointed with himself and unhappy that he hadn't worked hard enough to achieve massive career success. He added that he hadn't really been that successful. I said, *"The next time you find yourself thinking in this way, take a very long, slow look at your son and daughter. Then ask yourself how successful you've been."*

He was stunned into silence for a moment. What followed was an overwhelming feeling of love for his children. As a truly devoted father, he'd allowed himself to forget about how much joy and happiness existed in his life already.

This is just one poignant example of how we all at times think ourselves 'down'. Unhappy people tend to be brilliant at this. Happy people recognise when they start to think like this, and have strategies that replace unhelpful thoughts with more empowering ones. They usually do this without even realising it. It is second nature to them. It can become second nature to you, too.

Happy people tend to remember to be happy. They fully appreciate what they have already. Unhappy people simply don't do that, they don't see any good in what they have, and they forget what being happy is.

Unhappy people don't know exactly what they want, just something 'better'. Invariably, they allow their unhelpful thinking patterns to focus repeatedly on what's wrong with their life. What's wrong with their body. They're too fat, too skinny, too tall, too short. Their nose is too pointed. Their breasts are too small. Their fault lists are often very long indeed.

The mistake they make is never questioning the real reasons for their unhappiness, which is the first step towards unlearning it. The true underlying cause of unhappiness is often related to the amount of time they allow themselves to think about what's wrong. They take their negative thoughts far too seriously. It never occurs to them that by thinking so much about what they've put on their fault lists they guarantee they will feel worse about themselves. Concentrating on what is bad never makes you feel better.

- How often do you allow yourself to think unhelpful thoughts that deprive you of feeling happier right now?
- What are the most unhelpful thoughts you tend to repeat to yourself regularly? Write them down.

In so many cases, the root cause of a person's unhappiness is because reality refuses to conform to the carefully constructed fantasy that has been allowed to grow inside their mind. They keep feeding it with notions of the way things should be in their life. In many cases, their fantasy becomes their reality. And the deep unhappiness which pervades their entire life is in the gap between the real world and how they feel it should be.

This is a critically important point. Everybody does it at times. But unhappy people tend to allow it to dominate their thinking. And unhappy people are likely to withdraw from other people, spending a lot of time on their own, so they do a lot of this type of thinking. When you drill down a bit deeper into why men and women are so unhappy, it's often their habit of over-analysing situations, coupled with a desperate desire to somehow fit reality to the fantasy they've created in their mind. It keeps them unhappy.

You can devote the rest of your life to complaining about what your life should be. Or you can make a simple decision to make the most of what it is on a day-by-day basis right now. Simply accept reality every day.

Dear Daughter
Your life is what it is. It is not the 'better' version you have created in your head.

When you learn to remind yourself daily that your life just is, over time you learn to accept it as being OK. Some days it will be less OK and on other days it will be a lot better than just OK.

deciding to be happy

Just suppose you could guarantee changing from being an unhappy person to a genuinely happy person in just eight hours. How would you spend that time? Would you think about your problems even more? Or would you concentrate on adopting strategies that made you feel better straight away? Effective people devote a higher proportion of their available time focusing on solutions, not their problems.

In his work as a stress counsellor, best-selling author Richard Carlson PhD 'cured' countless unhappy people quickly, simply by helping them to adopt new thinking strategies. He often told his patients, *"Being upset by your own thoughts is similar to writing yourself a nasty letter – and then being offended by that letter."*

How many people do you know who effectively do that every day of their lives?

It all starts with making a decision to be happy. This then becomes a priority in your life. You give it your attention every day. Carlson explained to his patients that how each of us feels, right now, in this moment, is a direct result of what we are thinking right now. Your thoughts create your emotions. They are linked directly. Unhappiness is an emotion, triggered by unhelpful thoughts. Without those thoughts, you cannot feel unhappy. Unhappiness simply cannot exist.

Thoughts are not real. They are part of your imagination. He compared dreaming to the thoughts we have while we're awake. We know our dreams are not real, but we seem to want to believe that our thoughts while we're awake deserve to be taken more seriously. They don't. Just because you thought them, doesn't mean they are accurate or correct.

Unhelpful thoughts repeated over a long period can have a devastating effect on anyone's well-being. And it's totally exhausting. So many suffer from perpetual self-critical patterns of thinking. These evoke deep and often painful emotions which trigger stomach-churning reactions. In many cases, they create a vicious emotional circle of pain and suffering. What we are unhappy about becomes what we think about the most.

Robert Holden PhD describes negative emotions such as guilt and anger as guests who often visit even though they have not been invited to come and stay. The same thoughts go round and round in your head, never getting resolved. Learn to recognise when unhelpful thoughts visit you, and invite them to leave. Mentally say, *"Oh, so it's you again. Please leave. I don't have time for you today."*

meet the 'hyper-happys'

On the other hand, pretending to be happy all the time won't make you happy. In fact, it could prolong your unhappiness. That's precisely what particularly unhappy people do.

Genuinely happy people are appealing to others. Unhappy people are less so. Far less so. Extremely unhappy people know this and will often go to extraordinary lengths to fool themselves and others into believing they are happy. And in many cases it's because they so desperately want to appear appealing to others.

Really unhappy people can be spotted quite easily when you know what to look for. I call them 'Hyper-Happy'. They have perfected the illusion of looking and behaving in ways that they believe represent happiness. It's usually too much. They are too 'up'. Too often. They don't seem to have down days. They are always wearing their 'happy face'.

Party animals are an extreme example of the 'Hyper-Happy' type. Their obsessive, frenetic pursuit of pleasure, fuelled by large quantities of alcohol, recreational drugs, risky adrenaline-producing activities, and a one-night stand mentality, are in most cases a 'front' for deep unhappiness and inner turmoil. You will never meet a happy alcoholic who's still drinking, or a happy drug user. But they can be so good at making you believe they are. They are hedonistic stimulation junkies. 'More' is never enough. Even so, they always focus on wanting 'more' now. Surely that would make them happy? More of the latest designer clothes, a better job, more money, more expensive holidays, a newer car; then they would be happy. But it doesn't work.

Think about it: truly happy people really don't need to get 'high' when they are high on life already.

Yet, to the uninitiated, Hyper-Happys can appear exciting, dangerous and intoxicatingly appealing. And anyone who's not as happy as they'd like to be is often attracted to these types in the mistaken belief that some of this exciting happiness will rub off on them. It doesn't. Hyper-Happys are so self-obsessed they constantly feed off others, who inevitably end up getting used, abused and discarded. Alternatively, once the Hyper-Happy has you hooked, they drop the pretence, reverting to their real behaviour: namely being unhappy. They were happy when they met you, but now they're not, so it must be your fault. And that blame is often sufficient justification to make their target's life a misery. They effectively say, *"I am not happy, you haven't made me happy. Therefore, it is your fault I am not happy. And you are going to pay. I will then be happy."* It is flawed logic, but it's the best they've been able to figure out. After all, nothing else has worked.

These unhappy Hyper-Happys are convinced that somebody else and 'better' circumstances will miraculously transform them into being happy, 'someday.' The trouble is the 'somebody else' always fails, the 'better circumstances' don't seem to arise (nor do they make any effort to improve their circumstances), and 'someday' never comes. It's more of a happiness mirage: always somewhere in the distance, out there on the horizon.

Truly happy people on the other hand, may look really boring by comparison. At least at first glance. Their happiness is inside. And it doesn't always show in the ways described above. But it is visible in their everyday lives.

happiness heartbeat and habits

We all have what I call a 'happiness heartbeat'. It's an 'upbeat' for happy types and a 'downbeat' for unhappy people.

During periods of great joy, the happiness heartbeat of happy folk may beat more quickly. At other times, a deep, calm contentment permeates throughout their entire body. They are at peace with life. The heartbeat is slow and regular . . . and still upbeat. It doesn't need feeding by external factors. In fact, genuinely happy people don't need loads of 'stuff' to make them happy. They are happy already. Because they understand what 'enough' means to them, they don't bother consuming or buying the latest fashions or unnecessary faddish toys. Able to delay gratification, they also benefit from the added advantage of enjoying everything twice: once while looking forward to it (which costs nothing), and again from the actual experience.

Happy people are open to new experiences, new ideas and new people. How open are you to anything new? If not, why not? What if you decided to stop deciding why things are not a good idea? Say *"yes"* to more opportunities, just for the hell of it. And just see what happens. (I'm not suggesting you do anything dangerous or reckless though.)

Above all, happy people know that happiness begins

on the inside and radiates outwards. That's why they attract so much into their lives. Unhappy people believe fervently that happiness is outside, and must be given to them.

For happy people, looking after themselves is a priority. They know that food, exercise and getting enough sleep are critical to their sense of well-being. They make a personal commitment to do what it takes to be physically, mentally and emotionally fit. They schedule quality time to do this each and every week. They always have enough time to do what is important to them.

Genuinely happy people don't overeat and don't indulge excessively in recreational drugs or alcohol. They don't need to. They know that fast food slows them down. So they avoid it. When they are feeling a bit 'down', they also know that the best way of getting themselves out of it is to do something – anything. They don't just sit around the house, moping. They act.

They know how to have real fun and are able to lose themselves in 'play'. It's part of looking after themselves. By ensuring they maintain a healthy work/life balance and manage their energy and stress levels, they don't burn themselves out. They know when to stop. They also know instinctively that being active makes them feel good, whether or not they are aware of the physiology of physical exercise. We feel better after exercise because it releases endorphins into our bloodstreams. These are natural chemicals that serve to make us feel good and positive. They know that their body achieves what their mind believes.

Happy people are action-orientated and know that even the most outstanding athletes don't win all of the time. By doing more, they inevitably end up getting more and better results. And they are able to set realistic goals and be happy with the results. Not all of these results will be outstanding, but they increase the likelihood that some will be.

Happy people manage to preserve their playfulness, joy and enthusiasm. They don't care if they're not 'good' or accomplished at what they enjoy. They like themselves and feel comfortable with the person they have become over the years.

They are open to the idea of seeing how something works out without requiring a guaranteed outcome from the very beginning. They blame no one and know they can achieve almost anything if they apply themselves to it. Even if they fail, they will have gained something in the attempt. Happy people also laugh a lot. Often at the most ridiculous things. They see the absurdity in everything. And they are not afraid to look or act ridiculous themselves from time to time. They feel good about themselves, they are not too worried about what others think.

They have learned to enjoy the 'now'. Happiness is made up of lots of little moments. They don't expect to feel joy all the time. They go with the flow, accepting reality and life for what it is, not what it could or should be. They don't always need to be right, and willingly accept that they don't have a monopoly on all good ideas. They listen to the opinions and views of others without feeling threatened. They are also open to feedback, which they take without resorting to defensiveness.

They become what they do and what they think about. They have 'good intentions' in everything they do and wish harm on no one.

They always look for, and see, the good in others. Without needing to keep score, favours are given freely with little or no expectation of 'repayment'. Happy people are always happy for other people's success, and are proactive about helping others to feel happy. That in itself makes them happier, too. They always seem to have time for others and actively collect friends and happy memories. They are generally relatively uncom-plicated. What you see is what you get. They have no hidden agenda and don't feel the need to impose rules on anyone else. If they have to reprimand someone, they do it respectfully, kindly and in private.

They refuse to beat themselves up emotionally and just concentrate on being and doing the best they can. At the same time, they don't squander their own time with people who consistently drain them. They firmly but politely minimise their interactions with nega-tive people. They have learned to protect themselves against toxic people and poisonous influences.

Generally, they feel good about themselves and who they are, regardless of what shape or size they may be. If that shape or size starts to bother them enough, they accept the responsibility to do something about it.

These are the people who love their jobs and would probably do it for free because they aren't driven by money. Even when they don't love their jobs, they accept their situation and do their best without com-plaint. Prepared to give more than they gain, they in-variably find they receive more than they expect.

And when it comes to love, even though they may have been hurt in the past, they aren't afraid to love unconditionally. The potential gain is worth more to them than the possible pain.

For happy people, life is easier. Less stressful. They're not overly suspicious, they don't make de-mands of others, they don't make mountains out of molehills. They don't major in minor things. Little things don't matter. It may have become a cliché, but they really do see the glass half full and not half emp-ty. They don't feel the need to say bad things about anyone.

Every happy person I have ever met likes them-selves and they have learned that when they feel good about themselves, just about everything around them takes on a more pleasant appearance.

Everyone can make a decision to be happy right now – in this moment.

If it helps, create a fuller list in a journal. In really simple terms, if you want to be happier, do a lot more of what happy people do, a lot less of what unhappy people do. Develop these habits from today.

what you need to know about:

being kind

Kindness is so uncool, isn't it? And kind people are weak. Or are they? Suppose you are feeling really grumpy. How easy would it be to take out that grumpiness on any innocent bystander? Perhaps someone you claim to care about. By contrast, how strong would someone need to be in order to ensure that they didn't let their grumpiness infect that same innocent bystander? Being grumpy to people who are innocent is simply self-indulgent and disrespectful no matter how you try to justify it.

Practising kindness and compassion is far more difficult, especially if or when you are stressed, tired or irritable. It can require a lot of effort, commitment and self-discipline not to spread how bad you feel to those who don't deserve to suffer. It really is so much easier not to bother. Just bite off the head of anyone who comes within snarling distance of you. How appealing do you think this type of behaviour is? Do it regularly and you will lose friends. It's as simple as that.

Is your bad temper what you really want others to remember about you?

In his book, *Why Kindness is Good For You*, author David R Hamilton PhD cites a study of 10,047 young people aged 20 to 25 from 33 different countries. The research found conclusively that kindness was more attractive than good looks or financial prospects. This applied to men and women. In short, being kind makes you more appealing to others. The personal health and well-being benefits to yourself are also quite compelling, as we will discuss as part of this Emotional Core component.

what is kindness?

The other three pillars of your Emotional Core, self-esteem, attitude and happiness, are mainly about what is inside you. Your attitude will, of course, have an impact on others, and your happiness may be contagious, but these effects are a by-product (albeit an important by-product) of your emotional fitness level. Kindness, on the other hand is outer-directed. It's about others. It's the way you express your emotions to yourself and everyone you know and meet. It is a point of view that effectively says, *"This person exists. They deserve my attention, my respect and even my support."* Whoever they may be.

Who do you know who you would describe as kind? What do they do that makes you think that way about them? I'll bet it involves how they treat everyone they meet, not just those who are 'important'. A true act of kindness so often creates a deep connection with the recipient of that kindness. It means even more to the recipient when the giver has no personal agenda. They are just giving with no desire or expectation of anything in return from that person. Kind people benefit in other ways. So, how kind are you: to yourself and others?

you first

How much do you criticise yourself? How often do

you tend to say negative things to yourself that you would never dare say to anyone else? Why do you do this? Putting yourself down is never kind to yourself, even if you've managed to fool yourself into believing it's a way of ensuring others don't think you have an overinflated ego. Attacking ourselves, before we give anybody else the chance to, is a common behaviour amongst people who have yet to learn that being kind to yourself is an essential element of being kind to others. You are not more deserving of criticism than others.

Before you can be kind to others, you must be kind to yourself. Being kind to yourself is not just about the way you treat yourself emotionally. It is about being kind to yourself physically, as well. If you were a high-performance car, how well would you run on low-quality fuel? Pretty poorly. Stuffing our faces with junk food is not an act of kindness to ourselves. Too many late nights followed by early mornings may be great fun at times, yet an ongoing lack of sleep is not being kind to yourself either.

It's a cliché, but often those who truly value their health are those who have lost it. Looking after your physical body makes sense on a logical level – but why is it that so many of us have been conned into believing that the best way to have fun is to do harm to our bodies?

As we discussed in an earlier chapter, millions run their most prized possessions, their bodies, on low-quality, although highly-convenient, rubbish. Fast food makes you slow. Poor quality food really does make you sluggish. What you eat and drink affects your mood and emotional well-being. Eat and drink crap and you'll feel like crap.

And how often do you wake up feeling exhausted in the morning? How late do you go to bed? Our bodies require sleep. Living on just a few hours of it is not a sign of strength. Constant tiredness, even among the young, is now extremely common. It affects the speed and clarity of our thinking. And treating your physical body unkindly affects your moods, emotions and general sense of well-being. Everything is linked.

now others

Think about how all of this unkindness you are showing yourself affects you. How likely would it be that someone running their lives in this way would be capable of kindness and be compassionate to others? It's not that likely, is it?

Looking after yourself properly (which isn't the same as being narcissistically self-obsessed) actually increases the likelihood that you'll treat others with more kindness. Think of the people you know who are not kind. They are almost certainly self-obsessed, selfish and inner-directed, sometimes in the extreme, aren't they?

why bother?

Male or female, just about everyone craves intimacy, kindness and being cared for. *"We are actually genetically wired to be kind. This is why it is good for us. And it is also why, when we don't show kindness, or compassion, gratitude or forgiveness, it stresses our nervous systems and is not so good for our health."* writes kindness expert David R. Hamilton PhD.

Being kind to others makes us feel good too. It's a loop. The health benefits include alleviating the symptoms of depression, hurt, stress, anger and anxiety. Doing good and being good also improve self-esteem. This is another example of how the components of our Emotional Core work together to nourish our overall well-being.

There is a clear link between how happy you are and how kind you behave. Happy people are nice to others, and being nice to others reinforces our happiness. There's that loop again.

A positive, caring attitude has also been found to lead to a longer life. Not only that, kindness is absolutely free. If you're prone to feeling a bit down or depressed occasionally, the most effective way to get you out of it, is to do something kind or helpful for somebody else. Without any expectation of anything in return. Doing so also gives you more energy, which in turn helps you feel more optimistic. Our brain produces the hormones serotonin and dopamine when we are kind. These natural chemicals act on our brains by also improving our optimism. Optimism in turn tends to make us more generous – not necessarily with money, but generous with our time and energy. These are all qualities that make you more appealing to others.

By learning to be kinder and more gentle with yourself, you start to radiate those qualities to those around you. When you understand the bigger picture of kindness, it isn't about you, it's about helping others feel great about themselves. Which doesn't just help them, it lights you up inside, too. People pick this up about you, even if they are not consciously aware of it. The kindness feedback loop is very real and incredibly powerful.

Perhaps it's because random acts of kindness don't tend to make the news, so they stand out in real life. It's a sad reflection of our society's priorities that the more uplifting aspects of human behaviour invariably get pushed into the shadows by the news media, in favour of a constant stream of cruelty, brutality and inhumanity.

how to be kind and compassionate

Think briefly of all the people who have done you wrong, cheated or deceived you. Perhaps you even hate some of them. When you hate somebody else, it only hurts you. Many people find it very difficult to let go; our bruised egos refuse to 'let them get away with it'. So we hold on to those deep, painful emotions. We so often fail to realise that forgiveness is a liberating experience. To forgive someone doesn't mean you have to like them or make friends with them. Forgiveness helps you. It helps you to become less resentful. It clears away dark clouds from the past.

Who could you forgive for whatever they did to you in the past? May be an absent parent? Do it today and notice how a great weight gets lifted from your shoulders. Forgive them whilst expecting nothing in return. They may not understand, they might not even care, but that's OK. You're doing it to be kind to yourself.

Most people are doing the best they can. So learn to be more patient and tolerant. Just because someone may fall short of your standards, it doesn't make them a bad person. Spot people doing good things and let them know you noticed. Help more people in your life to feel special about themselves. Learn how to let out what makes you special so others appreciate you more. The simplest and most effective way to do that is to help others let out their specialness first.

Try developing another new habit of doing at least one kind deed every day without the recipient of your kindness or anybody else knowing. Notice how it makes you feel so much better about yourself. It is the most delicious feeling in the world to know that you've made somebody else's life on that day just a little bit better, without needing to be recognised or thanked for it. In a journal you might like to write down what you did and how these kindnesses made you feel about yourself. Rereading these notes in the future may help you remember what a good person you are.

Make a decision to give at least three genuine and sincere compliments to family, friends, colleagues and even some strangers every day. Never be afraid to give sincere compliments. People of both sexes love to hear them. Imagine you've just met somebody – let's say a woman at a party – and she says to you: *"Wow, I love your outfit – you look fantastic!"* You immediately warm to her, right? She has made you feel good about yourself. She is a Tonic personality, rather than a Toxic one. The joy in spreading such good feelings to others is infectious once you get used to it. Giving compliments without fear is liberating. Very, very few people will ever be offended. Give it a go.

Boys and young men can be very insecure especially around females they really like. Don't let their confident image fool you. A compliment doesn't have to be anything physical (which might be misinterpreted as a sexual come-on). Tell a guy if you honestly think they are really funny, bright, have a great smile etc. Just like you, they want to know they are OK too.

Devote yourself to becoming a gold medal Olympic listener. Really listen. If you have to, bite your tongue until the other person finishes. That's not to say that you become everybody's 'audience'. Listening makes people feel special. Give people your undivided attention. Make them realise what they're saying is important to you. Encourage others (especially the quiet types) to open up. Be interested. Look for the good in others and you'll find it in yourself.

Notice the 'invisible' people. I once read an article about a homeless man who talked about the worst aspects of his situation. He didn't want to beg, so he spent hours trying to sell copies of *The Big Issue*, a newspaper now sold by homeless people all over the world. In the article, the homeless man remarked that over 90% of the people who passed by would look through him as if he wasn't even there. I'm not saying you must always buy a copy, but see the person. Acknowledge the existence of everyone. A smile costs nothing. In Africa, there's a traditional greeting *"I see you."* This means far more than *"Hello."* It's about recognising and respecting that person at a much deeper level.

Imagine what it must be like to be the other people in your life. Appreciate the difficulties they experience. Empathise and understand. Always practise good manners. Simply say *"Please"* and *"Thank you"* more often. This is such basic stuff that gets ignored by so many. Yet politeness is free.

penalties and risks of being 'too' kind

Can you be 'too' kind? Yes. Being a 'people pleaser' who is too accommodating and considerate can have a negative longer-term effect. Others may learn to take advantage of such generosity. You may be seen as 'weak' if they think you are prepared to say *"Yes"* to every request. Learn to say *"No"* when it's appropriate. Being kind is not the same as always agreeing to others' wishes.

Recognise and accept that you will be more appealing to some of the wrong people, but also to the right people. So be aware of the risks but don't let it stop you from improving the quality of life for those you know and care about. And listen more to your gut instinct. If you sense that someone is trying to take advantage of you, don't let them.

So, you might be thinking, if this is going to happen, doesn't it make sense to avoid being kind and compassionate in the first place? This way you protect yourself. No. The benefits of being a kind and compassionate person far outweigh any possible disadvantages.

Kind people have become something of a rarity in this dog-eat-dog world. Be that person. But gently insist that any other person in your life needs to be, too.

what I wish I'd known about:

relationships with others

"Anybody who thinks the world would be a better place if it were run by women doesn't remember high school." Madeleine Albright, former US Secretary of State.

friends and frenemies

It's only human for you to want to be popular, to feel included and appreciated within social groups, at school or within the workplace. On the one hand, you want to be independent, whilst on the other you want to 'belong'. You may want your own unique identity but also feel the desperate need to wear the same clothes and behave like your 'coolest' friends. But knowing how to fit in without sacrificing one's own unique identity can be challenging at times.

I used to keep chickens. It was fascinating to observe their behaviour. Within all chicken flocks there's a pecking order. The more powerful chickens use their beaks to literally peck at the less powerful. It is cruel and painful for the victims. Some chickens die as a result. (It's worth remembering that all chickens are female!) Among humans there is also a pecking order. You need to know how it works. Knowing where you are in the pecking order amongst your friends can be very enlightening.

Insecure, needy people with poorly developed Emotional Cores are far more likely to accept the unacceptable and are usually at the bottom of a pecking order. To them, any friendship is better than no friendship. They crave being part of any social groups, cliques and gangs. Their desire to 'belong' becomes far more important than who they hang out with, and how much they even like or respect their so-called friends.

In some schools and colleges it's even seen as 'normal' to be picked on (pecked), bullied, humiliated, teased or frozen out of social circles. The antics of those who rule these social circles are accurately described in the excellent book for the parents of teenage girls *Queen Bees and Wannabes* by Rosalind Wiseman. Queen bees will do just about anything to get to and stay at the top of a pecking order. These 'mean girl frenemies' rule their social circles by fear and intimidation.

Personally, I think describing these young women as 'queen bees' is disrespectful for the poor humble bumble bee! A more accurate, but totally politically incorrect description for these mean girls could be PLBs; Pretty Little Bitches. And if they aren't pretty, the 'p' can also stand for pathetic, pitiful or petty. Which is what they so often are.

Who do you know who would qualify as PLBs? Do you think they have high or low self-esteem? Do they have a healthy attitude towards life and other people? Are they genuinely happy individuals? And how kind are they? The chances are they possess few if any of those qualities. They almost certainly have non-existent, or very poorly developed Emotional Cores.

They often behave like this because they believe if they can put others down, it some how lifts them up. It does, if no one around them knows their dark secret: namely their deep feelings of inadequacy.

Remember that any individual with a well-developed Emotional Core doesn't feel the need to mistreat anyone for any reason. Realise that in the future you will be mistreated by others; it's how you deal with those situations that will define you as a woman. So, learn to observe the behaviours of those in your social circles. Mean and dangerous men are dealt with in a lot more detail in a later chapter. But by paying a bit of attention, you will quickly learn how to recognise (and avoid) the meanest women too. These are some of the telltale signs. As a fun quiz, think of the worst PLB you know, then fill in the box for each quality they possess:

- ☐ Says or writes mean, cruel, vicious and even untrue statements about other people by text, email or posted on social websites. It's only a matter of time before they'll do it to you (although it could be happening behind your back already).
- ☐ Shares secrets or disrespects the privacy of others.
- ☐ Shares personal photos of others that could be used to harm the reputation of those in the photos.
- ☐ Teases, bullies or humiliates people in front of others.
- ☐ Does anything that's designed to make someone feel bad or worse about himself or herself.
- ☐ Gives others the silent treatment, and/or encourages others to collectively do the same against certain individuals.
- ☐ Rolls their eyes when they hear anything they think is uncool or disagree with.
- ☐ They call people names. Everything from racist remarks to being called 'fat' or 'stupid'.
- ☐ When challenged about name-calling they respond with *"I was just joking."* Or *"Can't you take a joke?"* This is often accompanied by a sneer.
- ☐ Generally uses a lot of sarcastic comments.
- ☐ Says how much they 'hate' someone. This is a much stronger and more poisonous word than users believe.
- ☐ They always notice the bad in people. Or what's wrong about someone or something.

☐ They tend to be jealous or resentful of others.

☐ They are on a life mission to take revenge on others. Even if the victim hasn't done anything wrong.

☐ They seem to gravitate towards other mean people. It's true that misery loves company.

☐ They only want to associate with 'powerful' people or those who can be useful to them.

☐ They are into 'social climbing'.

☐ They convince themselves that reckless, disrespectful or irresponsible behaviour is somehow 'cool'.

☐ They think being rude (especially to strangers) is cool.

☐ They believe taking their grumpiness out on innocent bystanders is OK.

☐ You tend to feel a bit worse about yourself during and after you spend time with these people.

☐ They are only interested in their own well-being and refuse to consider the feelings of others.

☐ You feel intimidated by them.

☐ They see you as competition. They don't seem to know that you are never in competition with a true friend.

☐ They put on a show by trying to appear mean in front of others; they think it helps them feel more secure. They are just fooling themselves.

☐ They are dishonest. They are cheats, sneaks and tell lies 'all the time'. They are not to be trusted.

The bigger (and braver) question you need to ask yourself is this: how many of the qualities listed on the previous pages are you guilty of? Are you a PLB yourself? If so, ultimately you will lose more friends than you ever think you will gain.

Accept that at some point you will be the victim of lies being told about you. You will also be betrayed, humiliated, let down and will feel devastated by the actions of girls you think of today as being your closest friends. It happens. Sometimes, all it takes is a friend saying just one wrong thing to the wrong person at the wrong time. At that time, you may feel that your world is collapsing around you. It isn't. It just feels like that. What is far more important, is how you deal with those temporary setbacks.

Dear Daughter:
Whatever you observe, keep it to yourself.

As a skilled observer, you develop an 'inner eye' which provides you with a much clearer understanding of who are the most likely to let you down, give you the silent treatment, betray your trust or turn on you. In many cases, you'll see it coming and be better placed to protect those you care about too. There's more on this in the chapter about girl power.

being a true friend

It's been said that if you want real friends, the first thing you need to do is **be** a real friend. Think about the people you know who are never cruel and don't allow themselves to get sucked into idle gossip. What is it about them that impresses you the most? Eliminate any of the behaviours above and adopt the behaviours of those people you are most proud of, until they become a part of you.

Do you think you could ever be someone who never said or wrote mean things about anyone, ever? It isn't necessarily easy but nor is it impossible if you made the decision to make this part of who you choose to be in the future. It's OK to feel angry sometimes. That's normal. But it's never a good idea to send a text, an email or post anything on a social networking site that says anything mean about someone else. In a moment of anger, it can be so easy to say or write something you later regret.

Always, always pause and reflect before you press 'send'. Reread everything you write. Remember this; nothing is ever deleted on the Internet. A careless or angry remark by you could so easily come back to haunt you, perhaps in years to come. Nor is it a good idea to ever forward anything that's cruel or mean about someone else. Yes, it's incredibly easy to do. And it can be difficult not to, especially when you feel hurt by the behaviour of others. But just because you think everyone else does it, is a lousy reason to lower yourself to the level of someone with a weak Emotional Core.

> "High school will not define you. Many people make high school out to be amazing, and the truth of the matter is, it isn't. Not only that, in the grand scheme of life, high school (socially) is not that important. My best advice would be to not stress over all the ups and downs with friends and boyfriends/girlfriends in high school. Chances are, you won't stay in touch with many of your classmates, and the ones you do remain friends with, will not be a part of the drama that is high school." Jessie Marr (www.MomVantage.net)

meeting new people with confidence

As you enter adult life, having good contacts who can open doors for you will have an enormous impact on what opportunities open up to you. Therefore, who you get to know in the years to come is incredibly important to you regardless of what you may think at the moment. And starting right now.

However, the biggest problem most people face (and this includes even the most senior, highly experienced men and women) is that nearly everybody feels very uncomfortable about starting conversations with people they don't yet know. And walking into a room of strangers frightens the hell out of a lot of people. In my talks on this subject, I usually joke that it's the fault of our mothers because who hasn't had it drummed into them from an early age *"Don't talk to strangers! It's dangerous!"*

As we all get older, this is something we really need to rethink. We must all learn to talk to more strangers because it's good for business, our careers and our love lives (although clearly, going up to a stranger just for a chat late at night in a dark alley is not a good idea).

We all realise the need to meet new people, but often feel gut-wrenchingly awkward about doing it and will go out of our way to find ways to appear 'too busy' to initiate conversations. We don't know what to say. We worry about what people will think of us. We worry about being rejected, and, of course, there's 'no point' because we can't ever remember anybody's name anyway.

If this describes you – guess what? All of these 'afflictions' are more common than you would imagine. If you are a sufferer – trust me – you are in the majority. Therefore, there is nothing wrong with you.

Get over it. This is so important for your future success. Learn to become more comfortable meeting new people. It is a fundamental life skill that you will benefit from for many decades to come.

The most successful people are almost always the best connected. With excellent connections you will hear about employment opportunities first. You don't get to the top, other people put you there. As your career develops, qualifications and intelligence aren't always enough to reach the top or achieve your career goals. Your ability to relate and connect with others is just as important, if not more so. Every time you meet someone new, your access to potentially valuable new contacts is multiplied by the number of people they know.

When people think well of you, some may be prepared to recommend you. For others to do this, they need to know, like, trust, value and respect you as a woman. Why? Because no one these days can afford to put their own reputation on the line by recommending someone who will (or could) let them down.

Some like to believe that technology can and does replace the need to meet 'real' people. I don't agree. You can never fully replace meeting people face-to-face. Social online media is now so widespread, millions interact more with their 'friends' virtually than they do face-to-face. It feels 'safer'. I call it 'arms-length intimacy'. Use technology more to reconnect with more people you know in real life.

Today and tomorrow 'know-who' is and will be more important than 'know-how'.

If you're looking to meet someone for a more personal relationship, it's all about letting a large network know that you're available. So, from now on, before you go out, or attend your next party, decide not to spend all your time only with the people you know already. Promise yourself that you'll start at least one conversation with someone you don't yet know.

A great way to put yourself in the right frame of mind is to think of every stranger you ever meet, from today onwards, as having the potential to be your next best friend, whether they're male or female. So get out more. Just do it.

Here's your first task to improve your confidence. It's fun and you'll learn that it's so easy. Although you might feel a bit self-conscious at first. That will disappear really fast. When you see someone in the street, in a coffee shop or a bar put a big smile on your face. And just say *"Hello"* in a very warm, friendly and upbeat way as you pass them by. That's all you do. You don't have to stop to have a conversation with them. Just carry on walking. It's really that simple. Give it a go. Do it regularly. Make it part of your daily life. You'll discover that in most cases, they will smile back and say *"Hello"* too.

Making this part of how you interact with others will help you overcome any shyness or reluctance you might have about meeting new people. Set out to achieve a target to meet, say, three new people per day and increase this number as your confidence and/or expertise grows.

Walking into a room of strangers can be intimidating to anyone. If you feel particularly uncomfortable about it you're less likely to go out of your way to get into such a position. Avoiding rooms full of strangers may protect you from feeling uncomfortable, but it won't help you meet new people. When you do put yourself through such potential torture, it's very easy to give the situation far more attention and importance than it deserves. But keep in mind that you are not alone: a huge proportion of people feel uncomfortable around strangers. Odds are five out of every six people you see at any party feel equally uncomfortable.

Focus on putting other people at their ease. By choosing to act as a 'hostess', regardless of whether it's your party or not, you become actively concerned not with your own discomfort, but with ensuring the comfort of others. This helps you forget about your own feelings. Look for people standing on their own and set yourself the task of helping them to feel better about being there.

Dear Daughter
Talk less about yourself. Listen more to others. People will think you're great!

How confident you feel and how confident you look are not the same. You can appear confident. Learn to stand upright with your feet slightly apart. Don't fold your arms, or cover your mouth with your hand. Make eye contact with those around you and have a smile on your face – this doesn't mean you must grin like a Cheshire cat. Be welcoming, not intimidating. Send out signals that you would welcome a conversation with others. This will increase the likelihood it will happen. Stand up. Sitting down won't help you meet people. And finally, learn to enjoy yourself.

If you'd like to know more about this topic, download my **free** eBook *Meet Greet and Prosper* which part of this chapter has been based on. There's a link to it at www.TheSensibleUncle.com/MGP

what I wish I'd known about:

men

> *"Here's all you need to know about men and women: women are crazy, men are stupid. And the main reason women are crazy is that men are stupid."* George Carlin, comedian.

If men are of absolutely no interest to you, nor will they ever be because you prefer female company, you can skip the next few chapters (although some of what is discussed here applies to all relationships with men or women).

If men do interest you, answer this simple question: What are men **for**?

You'd be forgiven for saying *"It depends on the man!"* I've asked this question to countless women of all ages and backgrounds. Their answers are always interesting, sometimes hilarious, and occasionally unpublishable. However, *"for companionship"* is by far the top answer. In second place: *"for sex"*. Some women point out that men are not necessary for reaching an orgasm. Although one woman conceded that her vibrator cannot mow the lawn. Third place, and related to sex is *"for making babies"*. No woman has ever told me *"To pay for a lifestyle of my choosing."* Yet a lot of women unashamedly state that a rich man is high on their list of 'must-haves'. Perhaps it's worth spending at least a little time clarifying in your own mind a serious answer to the above question.

Here's something else to ponder: how much serious thought have you ever given to what it must be like to be a man in the 21st century? Do you think it's easier, or more difficult than being a woman? If your instant reaction was that it's easier to be a man (as so many women still believe) why is it that suicide is the biggest cause of death amongst men aged 15-35? Furthermore, more men than women get killed doing dangerous work supporting their families. And statistically, women live longer than men.

I distinctly remember having a conversation with the wife of a friend of mine. At a dinner party, in front of friends, she constantly complained about him for not doing everything she demanded of him. Eventually, I'd had enough of her public attacks and reminded her that the moment she got married, she stopped work. She was able to make that choice. She wanted to start a family. She did so. While she had the luxury of making these significant life decisions, he on the other hand, was stuck in a job he hated in order to support her and a growing family. His dream was to work in professional theatre. He was prepared to sacrifice his own dreams in order to allow his wife to live hers. She didn't like it, but knew it was the truth.

What it's like being a guy is probably not what you think, even though everyone is led to believe we live in a man's world. It really doesn't feel that way for millions of young men today.

Good men (as opposed to jerks), take their responsibilities and commitments very seriously. If settling down with a man one day is part of your life plan, make it a priority to find a good man. Part of that is knowing how to identify them. They are not always 'hot' at first sight.

Picture the scene: a group of five drop-dead gorgeous young women in a swanky London bar. Long legs, short skirts, perfect hair, teeth and flawless make-up. A quiet, respectful, 'nice' guy approaches one of the women and tries to initiate a conversation. I watched from a distance eager to see what happened next. She blew him off almost instantly. He had the sense to retreat. As soon as his back was turned, she made the 'L' sign with her thumb and forefinger and almost spat the word *"Loser!"* to her friends who all laughed like hyenas in agreement. What they didn't even stop to consider was just how much courage that guy had needed to do what he had done. (Not to mention what a lucky escape he'd had not getting involved with someone who had perfected the illusion on the outside of being so beautiful, yet inside she was such a cruel, shallow woman.)

is he for you?

How quickly do you decide whether a guy is your 'type', or not? Not tall enough, wrong hair colour or wrong brand of jeans? If you are looking for a long-term man in your life, be very careful indeed about how you judge (or instantly dismiss) the type of partner you think you want, and who you don't. Some women are world-class at choosing the 'wrong guy'. And they make the same mistakes over and over again. Don't be one of those women.

Are your preconceived notions of what makes a man 'of interest', more or less likely to lead to disappointment or emotional hurt for you? Do you attract disrespectful men, while blowing off genuine (and often quieter) men who actually want to treat you well? Gregarious men may appear more interesting on the outside, but as you'll discover in years to come, they are not always good for you.

So, don't be too quick to decide on your 'type'. Be a lot more open-minded.

Most women seem to agree that they go through a phase of being 'boy crazy'. Usually this starts mid-teens. Unfortunately this also coincides with the time when most boy-men of the same age are at their most obnoxious and least appealing: loud, uncouth, crass, cruel, aggressive, incredibly immature (even though they believe the opposite is true), disrespectful of all forms of authority and particularly disrespectful of young women. They lack even the most basic social skills and manners. With raging hormones, in particular testosterone, they may desperately crave female interest (and the more naked the better), yet possess little or no knowledge about how to be someone who any self-respecting female would be interested in spending time with. It's no wonder young women find older guys more interesting and a lot more mature. But with that maturity comes an expectation of sexual favours that could be more than a younger girl is prepared for or willing to offer.

Here is a crucially important piece of information you need to know about most guys in their teens and twenties. At first, you rarely get to see the real person. Instead you see a 'pretend' man. Almost all young guys pretend to be who they think a man should be. When they pretend well, they appear cool. When they get it wrong, they come across as a jerk!

Before you complain that this makes it so difficult for a girl to identify genuine guys, stop and consider for a moment how impossible it is for guys to see a genuine woman behind all that make-up, hair and revealing clothing.

At this stage of life, with the least experience of the opposite sex, and the most curiosity, everyone is expected to make good choices.

Shy, quiet guys are in many ways the most genuine people and therefore the least likely to be 'losers'. Don't fall so easily for the confident-looking pretend guys. Invariably, quiet men are in awe of women and possess sensitivity that seemingly confident guys don't have, or even want to have. So don't be too quick to dismiss the quiet ones.

What qualities make most sense for you to look for in a man? And which ones don't really matter? Firstly, it doesn't matter whether he thinks and behaves just like you or not – as long as his thoughts and behaviours are not hateful or hurtful. Many successful couples are made up of very different individuals who complement each other. Similarly, don't reject out of hand a man who refuses to do everything you want from him. Ask yourself if your demands are reasonable. Keep in mind that a man who is prepared to say *"no"* to the unreasonable demands of someone (male or female) will make a better long-term partner than a doormat guy. Indeed, you would almost certainly grow to resent any man who accommodates your every whim. Subconsciously you will start to find him weak for giving in to you too much.

If you only take one thing from this chapter make it this: just because a man doesn't think and behave the same way as you, it does not make him a 'bad' man. The opposite also applies: just because you don't think and behave the same way as a man, it doesn't make you a 'bad' woman.

As straightforward as men are, it's hard for a chapter of this length to cover the entire subject of 'Men'. That said, if you want to be able to get on better with men, the next few pages will attempt to explain some of the key differences between how men and women think and behave. Of course they are generalisations, there are plenty of exceptions, but these points are still useful.

how men and women talk and think differently

There's the story of the young boy who goes to his dad and asks him a question. The dad is preoccupied reading the newspaper. He suggests that the boy go and ask his mother instead. The boy then says in sheer frustration, *"But dad – I don't want to know **that** much."*

Women often accuse men of not listening. That's not true in so many cases. However, the real problem for men is that there is often so much to listen to.

Generally speaking, men don't talk as much as women. Two guys can go fishing for the day and barely speak to each other but have a brilliant time together.

Here's a key difference between men and women: when a man is silent he is usually (but not always) happy and contented. When a woman is silent she usually isn't happy or contented. Therefore, if you are with a man who is quiet, don't assume he is unhappy, as you would be if you were quiet.

Maybe it's a prehistoric thing. When a man went out to hunt, he couldn't chat to his companions and stalk animals at the same time. It would frighten away the animals. Silence was therefore essential.

Men 'report talk' while women 'rapport talk', according to Deborah Tannen, author of *You Just Don't Understand*. Report talking is about saying as much as possible with the least number of words. Using the correct word is important to men. It demonstrates clarity of meaning and focus. Short sentences are manly. Like this one.

For a man, the telephone is a tool to exchange facts. It is not for gossiping for hours on end. Women see such conversations as strengthening the connections in a relationship. It's rapport talk. Historically, while men were away hunting, the women would look after children and each other. Building rapport, trust and closeness with people was therefore an essential part of her history, too.

Women have no difficulty doing lots of things at the same time. That includes conversation topics. Women are so good at conversation that they can even run separate ones simultaneously. As a woman, you already know this. Men get totally confused. It's very common for a man to think, *"What is she talking about now? I'm completely lost."* Men really can't keep up.

Men tend to function best when they do just one thing at a time. And that includes sticking to one point while talking. Because men know this, men tend not to interrupt other men. But women can't contain themselves. They will bring up new points all the time – but they don't see it as interrupting. To a woman it's proof you're engaged, and want to be a part of the conversation.

When men are interrupted, they just forget what they were trying to say.

I have a friend with five sisters. It's no surprise he became a professional speaker. He has found the perfect job. He can talk uninterrupted for an entire hour. And get paid for what he thinks.

Men do talk a lot of course – but most of it is to themselves internally. Men are constantly thinking about solutions to problems, personal or work-related ones. A man can be very happy quietly thinking about his stuff. The blank 'gazing in the fire' type of expression on his face doesn't mean he's upset.

Here lies another problem. When you see a man doing this, you might assume he's 'doing nothing'. So you try to talk to him. To him, it's an interruption. To compound things you may decide to give him things to do – because you believe he's not doing anything. But to him, he is busy with something important and you are forcing him to do something else.

Many women think out loud. Men tend to do this a lot less than women. It often drives men crazy to have to listen to a constant stream of what a lot of women may think are 'interesting' or 'essential' additional details.

To communicate well with a man, be direct. Say what you think concisely. Don't waste your time trying to be subtle, you're only likely to get annoyed or irritated with him for not understanding what you really meant. And he won't have a clue what you're going on about.

For example, you're walking along the street with a guy. You ask, *"Would you like a coffee?"* He says *"No thanks."* That's the end of the subject to him. He really did not realise that you were politely telling him that you wanted a coffee, either because you're thirsty or because you'd like to have an enjoyable conversation with him.

To give you an idea of how dumb or naïve a young guy can be, in my youth, I was occasionally invited by dates to go back to her place for a coffee. I didn't drink coffee then, so I'd decline. It took quite a while for me to realise what else I may have been turning down.

Women often expect men to fully understand the meaning behind their subtlety. After all, every woman would understand... But, men are not women.

For example, let's take the phrases *"could you"*, *"would you"*, *"would you like to"*. To a young man, he will take what you say literally. (Older men have learned this lesson.) To a young guy, what you've said sounds as though you're giving him a choice. He doesn't know they are not choices but requests. However, in response to such questions, a man may say *"yes"* because, being literal, yes, he 'could' do it. He hasn't said he will do something, and certainly not right now. However, a woman is likely to perceive his *"yes"* as a commitment to doing it, and possibly to acting on it immediately. If he then doesn't do what she believes he promised to do, she will feel he is unreliable or lazy. In turn, he becomes frustrated and irritated by her 'wrong' interpretation of what she thought she heard.

Be careful about asking a man a lot of questions. He'll feel criticised. Ask the same questions more than once and he will feel you are nagging him. Men hate to feel nagged.

In John Gray's book *Men are From Mars Women are From Venus*, he describes how men have the capacity to put their problems on hold. Women don't tend to do that. When a woman wants to talk about her problems, she just wants to be heard. A huge number of men still don't know this. These men will jump in, and with the best of intentions, offer unasked-for solutions. And probably be offended or annoyed when these pearls of wisdom are ignored or rejected by a woman. Therefore if you want to talk about your problems with a man, it's very important that you say up front that you don't want or need him to tell you what to do.

Some men will genuinely think that it's a waste of his time listening to you if you don't want a solution. Therefore, you need to convince him that just being heard by him is important to you. And tell him that he really doesn't have to do anything else. If he's a particularly receptive guy, train him to listen without interrupting and then get him to say, *"So, what have you decided to do about it?"* If you've trained him really well, he'll listen some more and then, as difficult as it is for him, he'll shut up and not offer you a solution.

These differences in conversation styles often cause huge problems between men and women. By understanding these basic differences, you will be at a real advantage in your dealings with men.

why it's unwise to overanalyse a man
Another key difference between men and women is how women are far more likely to overanalyse situations and conversations. Be careful that your opinions are never allowed to get turned into 'facts' about something or what someone meant. Men tend not to do this.

I have lost count of the number of times female friends have come to me over the years asking me to translate the meaning behind various things their husbands or boyfriends may have said or done that has upset, annoyed or irritated them. In many cases (but not all), once they've explained what happened (by answering a lot of precise questions from me), they realise that their man has actually been incredibly supportive of them. It can be so easy to misinterpret and then make inaccurate assumptions based on what you misunderstood.

Assuming he's not a selfish, insensitive jerk (if he is – what are you doing with someone like that?), any time you are upset by a man's behaviour, ask yourself this question, *"What was his intention when he said or did that?"* If you aren't sure, don't guess – ask him. If he was trying to do the right thing – his intention was good. His poor choice of words or phrases (from your point of view) should not negate his good intentions. Being upset or annoyed with him on those occasions would therefore be inappropriate unfair, and hurtful to you both.

"Men socialise by insulting each other, but they don't really mean it. Women socialise by complimenting each other, but they don't really mean it either!" Anonymous

banter

Unsophisticated alpha-males will use physical force, dressed up to look like its boisterous 'fun', in order to assert authority over another man. Men with more brain cells will often put down other men verbally when they are trying to assert their authority or masculinity. Men respect a man who demonstrates mastery in 'verbal combat' by the quickness of his wit.

When male friends get together, the closer they are as friends, the more insulting they will be to each other. If one guy insults another, he almost expects to be given a more 'hurtful' insult in return. This banter is a demonstration (to men at least) that their friendship is built on a solid foundation. Generally speaking, the more insulting a man is to another male friend, the more secure they feel in that friendship. If a guy ever steps over the line with a close male friend, by saying something 'too hurtful', the guy who has been hurt will quietly ask him to stop. And he will. And he'll usually apologise.

> **Important:** What you have just read only applies man-to-man. It very definitely does not apply to women who decide to take part in male banter.

Some women like men to think that they can be one of 'the lads', and decide to take part in male banter. Be very careful. You could end up getting upset. Here's why. Good banter among men invariably escalates. It quickly becomes extremely crass and cruel. Cruel words, even when they're harmless fun to a guy, could be deeply upsetting to you. Many men have been totally confused when one minute they're having great banter with a woman, and then out of the blue she bursts into tears 'for no reason'.

mocking men

If you are in a relationship with a man, or he just likes you a lot, cruel words will hurt him more deeply than you can imagine. And far more than he will ever show. Mocking a man in public or in front of his friends is even worse. If you are in a relationship with him, this type of humiliation may even lead him to dump you, especially if he has a strong Emotional Core. It is tantamount to issuing a death sentence to a relationship. If you feel the need to mock him 'because he deserves it', just get out of the relationship. It really won't last.

buying gifts for men

Generally speaking, the more practical the gift, the more it will be appreciated by a man. Anything you find cute, sentimental or romantic is probably not going to impress him very much, if at all. He might try to appear appreciative so as not to offend you, but he is almost certainly thinking, *"What the hell am I supposed to do with **this**?"*

> Him: *"How would you like your eggs darling?"*
> Her: *"Unfertilised"*.
> Dorothy Parker, writer and wit.

is he 'into you'?

Being blunt, if you're a reasonably good-looking woman, who looks after herself, he will be 'into you', at least sexually. If he's into you in any way he'll find ways to contact you. He'll call you. He'll text. However, he may be shy, so his contact may be more subtle. He'll find any excuse he can think of to talk to you, meet you or spend time with you. He may try to make it look like an accident. If he doesn't initiate any contact at all, then he's not into you. It's that simple.

But how can you tell if he's into you as a person? He'll ask you what you think and feel about stuff. He'll ask you for your opinions and even your advice.

However, if he doesn't ask you these things it doesn't mean he's not into you. It's possible that he's so nervous because he's **so** into you, he gets tongue-tied and reverts to what most guys do in such situations – he'll talk on a subject he knows the most about – himself.

To find out his true intentions, say in a low-key way, *"I'm curious. Why don't you ask me what I think about things?"* If he doesn't pick up on this, by starting to ask you questions, he may need to be consigned to history. Do make sure, though, that if he asks you what you think – have opinions.

how wise is it for you to be 'into him'?

Some guys put on a great show, but can be more trouble than they are worth. The dangerous ones are dealt with in the next chapter, but here's some wise advice from Katrien Van der Veere:

> *"Observe carefully how he behaves with different people in different situations. Be as objective as you can. How does he treat his own family such as grandparents and parents? How does he behave towards staff in restaurants, to kids, to animals, to really annoying people? How does he talk about his friends? How does he treat strangers? If or when he's drunk what is he like? What about when he's really angry (and what makes him angry?) When he's sad, stressed? How does he handle embarrassment? How often does he blame others when things don't work out to his liking? How compassionate and kind is he?*
>
> *"You can learn far more from how he behaves to others than how he behaves towards you. And it can tell you a lot about how he could treat you in the future. The same of course applies to your own behaviour towards him!"*

in and out of love

When we first start dating, our hormones are racing. It's so easy to project dream qualities onto a man that he doesn't actually possess. For instance, let's say he tosses a coin to a busker. You see him as unbelievably generous and wildly charitable. He pats a passing dog, you see him as kind, gentle and loving. He smiles at a child – he'd make a great father, and you want his babies. Stated like this it sounds crazy, but it doesn't feel that way at the time, does it?

During your lifetime, it's possible you will fall in and out of love numerous times. And various men may fall in and out of love with you. A break-up, whether initiated by you or by him, can feel devastating. All that time and emotional energy that's been poured into a relationship can seem wasted. But it's never wasted. Feeling deeply upset is proof that the relationship mattered to you.

If a man loves you but you don't feel that way towards him, be kind. Let him down with respect and consideration. Don't play games, or string him along.

A man who doesn't love you, isn't necessarily a bad man. (Although he might be a dumb one for passing up on such a great woman.) If he ends a relationship with you he obviously has his reasons. Accept it with dignity. Emotions often run deep. You may hurt like hell and feel that your world has ended. How you react to a break-up can tell you a lot about yourself. Reacting with anger or behaving vindictively or maliciously towards your ex demonstrates personality traits that could possibly have been the reason he broke up with you. Be honest with yourself. Identifying these flaws in yourself doesn't mean you are a bad person, but it does mean you need to change.

Regardless of the reasons for a break-up, always wish your ex future happiness. Especially if you believe he doesn't deserve it. Being the 'big' one, being the grown-up, actually helps **you** during the healing process after a break-up.

As we reach the end of this chapter, what follows are a few final thoughts on men:

- Men do not have telepathic powers when it comes to understanding your unmet needs, desires or requests. It may be obvious to you, but it isn't to him. Really.

- If a man tells you he doesn't know how he feels about something, it is highly probable that he is being totally honest with you. He's not hiding anything.
- Don't ask a man for advice and then get angry with him if he tells you something you didn't want to hear. That includes asking him if your bottom looks big in a particular outfit. If you think it looks big, it probably is.
- Men are not interested in hearing detailed accounts of conversations you have had with people they don't know. He will be turned off by even relatively short (to you), detailed, blow-by-blow accounts of 'she said this and then she said that'. After just five minutes he may even give up the will to live.
- If you really like a man, show him how much by never inviting him or insisting he goes shopping with you. The majority of men (not all) really hate shopping and can instantly come up with dozens of alternative ways they would rather spend their time. In particular, almost all straight men dislike clothes shopping. If a man agrees to go shopping with you, he is only doing it for what he considers a quieter life. He may deny this. But he is possibly lying to you. Shopping, for a man, is very rarely a hobby or an enjoyable way to while away a few hours at the mall. He will probably hate it.
- If you want to dress your man, remember he is not a Ken doll. If you can get him to go, it's likely he will want to park as close as possible, go directly to the precise store he needs, go to the shelf, quickly choose the product, try it on (if absolutely necessary), pay and go home. Men are simple creatures.
- Likewise, if a guy ever invites to you go on a fishing trip. Don't (unless you are a keen angler). You will probably hate it. You will be bored stupid. You will want to talk to him and that will spoil his fishing.

- Men tend to want their women to never change. Women expect their men to change. Don't ever try to change a man. You will only end up disappointed when he doesn't.

More than anything in the world, all men, like women, want to be noticed and appreciated sincerely. Learn to appreciate how men are different from women. These differences can be part of the fun when you're with a genuine man. However, sometimes men are not genuine. In fact, some can be quite dangerous. You must know how to spot them early. That's the subject of the next chapter.

"As an older woman you learn that life is never black and white. We've all been in destructive relationships. I was in one. But looking back, I remember with such clarity so many decades later, the setting, what I was wearing, the smells and what became the single most romantic moment in my entire life. That will stay with me until the day I die. So even in bad times, remember there are always opportunities for such life-affirming experiences. It's what helps mould your life as a woman." Anonymous woman (49).

"There's far more to life than men."
Anonymous

"Anonymous was a woman."
Virginia Woolf, English novelist

what I wish I'd known about:

dangerous men

Any man who ever slaps, punches or kicks you is dangerous. To you and perhaps to himself. Such attacks always have a habit of escalating. In extreme cases, you could end up getting seriously hurt, or even killed. A man subject to violent rages against you has deep-seated issues that are a threat to your safety.

If you are in a relationship with such a man, it is an abusive relationship. Leave the relationship, regardless of what you may think is 'good' about it. Especially if your friends are urging you to do so, too.

His pleas for you to forgive him for his violence and how much he claims to love you may sound painfully heart-felt. Don't fall for it. He is a danger to you. He is out of control. Indeed, you could be doing him a massive favour by ending the relationship. Only then will he be forced to face up to his problem and do something about it by seeking professional help. Perversely, the longer you stay with a violent man, the more you perpetuate the violence. He can carry on like he always has. As difficult as it might appear, get out.

"But I love him." You might say. No you don't. It's more likely that you are afraid of what he might do to you, or of being alone. If booze or other forms of recreational medications usually trigger his violence, he needs professional help. And you are **not** the person to provide it.

caught in a cycle

Never ever accept responsibility for his violence – even if he accuses you of being the reason he behaves in the ways he does. You are not the cause of his violence, he is. He has absolutely no excuse. Some women with low self-esteem fall into the trap of believing his accusations. They may justify his actions with the convoluted logic: *"If he gets this angry, it proves he must really care about me."* It is not unknown for some women to subconsciously provoke a man, in order to get this 'proof' of his love.

Realise that physical violence is illegal. Not only does he have no moral right to hit you, he has no legal right to, either. And this is a two-way street: it is just as illegal for you to slap, bite, scratch or punch a man. It seems socially acceptable to hear some women say, *"He must have deserved it"*, when they hear that a woman has assaulted a man. No, he didn't. Just as it is shocking for any man to say a woman 'deserved' to be beaten, it is unacceptable for a woman to say a man 'deserved' it. Violence perpetrated by either a man or a woman is never 'deserved' or justified.

Being bruised and bloodied by a violent man is bad enough, but these relationships devolve into something even worse; they become psychologically abusive too. They end up crushing the confidence and self-esteem of the victim, often to the point where she becomes a shadow of her former self. If you (or a friend) stay in such a relationship, it is almost always a sign of very low self-esteem. Abusive men seek that level of control over a woman. In their mind at least, they feel stronger when they force someone else to be 'weaker'. Invariably these men are emotionally bankrupt themselves.

"If it hurts, it's not love." Chuck Spezzanno PhD

Those who become involved in abusive relationships find themselves getting sucked into them. Misplaced loyalty, guilty thoughts of abandoning someone who 'needs' them, the desire to 'feel needed' or not believing you deserve anyone better are all thoughts that conspire to keep you in a bad relationship. It's the same with the widespread belief *"I can change him."* No, you can't. He has to want to change for himself, and chances are he won't. It's worth asking yourself, are you trying to change him just to increase your own self-esteem by proving that you could?

A woman with a well-developed Emotional Core would never allow herself to stay in a physically abusive relationship. More importantly, her emotional strength would allow her to recognise danger signals far sooner and get out of a relationship with someone before she got too tangled up in his issues.

Mothers are usually brilliant at spotting potentially dangerous boyfriends (many have personal experience from their own youth.) Unfortunately, as many mothers discover, saying anything to a daughter is a waste of time because she won't listen. In fact, the more parents disapprove, the more appealing the 'bad boy' boyfriend often becomes.

There are varying shades of 'bad'. Violent men are the easiest to spot. Looking at your black eye and bruised cheek in the mirror is quite a giveaway.

But other types of dangerous men can be far more difficult to identify. And they have the potential to be extremely harmful to your emotional long-term well-being.

If you are a particularly kind, loving, trusting, caring, sensitive woman who avoids confrontation, you need to be particularly vigilant about the men described over the next few pages.

These men actively target women who are prepared to trust (perhaps too much), accept the lies they are told and give these men the benefit of any doubts they might have about them because, on the face of it, they can appear so enticingly exciting, charismatic and charming. Indeed it's common for particularly kind people to feel guilty for even entertaining ideas that they are even being taken for a ride. Because a kind person thinks the best of others, he or she is unlikely to suspect they are being 'played'.

Unscrupulous 'takers' are fantastic at making you feel sorry for them (often when they absolutely don't deserve it). And he'll milk your generosity for as long as he can get away with it. It's all an act. And it is designed to deceive you. To him, you are merely his next victim. By the time you realise what's been going on, he has moved on. Here's how to be more alert, without losing the kindness that's so important to your Emotional Core.

men to recognise and avoid

The men we're describing here aren't always consciously aware of what they are doing, while some know exactly what they are up to. What you will find is that a lot of ice-cold men have perfected the illusion of appearing attractive and charming. But how do you tell the difference? Most women can't. The following could help you. One day (if you haven't already) you could meet men who exhibit the following personality traits:

- He has an extreme and grandiose sense of his own importance.
- He has an assumption of very high levels of his own talent, success, good looks and power even when these qualities are absent or would not be recognised by people who know him.
- Does he insist on excessive and constant admiration?
- Does he have a belief that he has a high degree of 'entitlement'? Because he believes he is special, he demands special treatment.

- Does he have extremely selfish, self-serving and arrogant tendencies?
- Does he have a readiness to take advantage of others in any ways he sees fit?
- Does he have an inability to feel empathy for others? Does he find it difficult to love others because a deep love for himself always comes first?
- Is he convinced that others are jealous of him?
- And would he be described as very demanding and controlling?

No, that does not describe **all** men. Seriously, everyone exhibits a few of these symptoms on occasion. However, if he has most or all of them, he very well may have narcissistic personality disorder (NPD). This is someone you want to avoid caring for, because he almost certainly won't care about you, no matter what he promises.

Other behaviours can tip you off that a man may not be all he seems, and his apparent interest in you as a person is merely a front.

At the beginning of the relationship he was on his best behaviour. He seemed to be your perfect partner. Now, as he has relaxed into the relationship with you, another side of him is being revealed.

In the safe environment, 'behind closed doors', he is now letting out years, or even decades, of anger that he has had to suppress until now.

He has intense, even violent, rages that seem to leap out of nowhere, and these alternate with periods when he acts perfectly normal and is very loving towards you. It makes it difficult to know where you stand with him.

Do you feel he is Dr. Jekyll and Mr. Hyde? Is he a loving, caring man one moment, and someone so vicious that you barely recognise him the next? Do you wonder which one is real? You hope it's a phase that one day will go away but shows no signs of doing so.

You walk on eggshells most of the time, knowing that, no matter what you say or do, it will get twisted and used against you.

You are blamed or criticised for just about every-thing that's wrong in the relationship, even when the criticism doesn't make much sense to you.

You question whether you are being the unreason-able one – as he constantly tells you.

You feel you are on an emotional roller coaster with high highs when things are incredible and fantastic and very low lows, consisting of feelings of despair, depres-sion and grief for the relationship you thought you had.

You find yourself concealing what you really think or feel because you're afraid of his possible reaction, and it just doesn't seem worth the confrontation, a horrible fight or hurt feelings that will inevitably fol-low. This has become so automatic that you have a hard time even understanding what you think or feel any more.

Are you afraid to ask for things in the relationship because you will be told you're too demanding or there is something wrong with you? Are you repeatedly told your needs are wrong or unimportant?

Do you feel nothing you do is ever right, or when you do manage to do what he wants he suddenly pre-sents new expectations? The rules keep changing and, no matter what you do, you can't win. Do you feel help-less and trapped every time this happens?

Are you constantly accused of doing things you didn't do and saying things you didn't say? Do you feel misunderstood a great deal of the time, and when you try to explain, he doesn't believe you or want to listen?

Are you constantly put-down, yet when you try to leave the relationship he tries to prevent you in a variety of ways? He tries declarations of love, or he promises to change, or he makes implicit or explicit threats such as, *"Nobody but me will ever want or love you."*

Do you have evidence of being lied to? Does he violently deny lying and deflect any conversation away from the topic when you raise it, or does he seem to manufacture accusations to 'prove' you are the liar? Do you feel you're being manipulated or controlled?

You regularly wonder whether you're losing your grip on reality because he is always putting you down, or denying your right to a point of view. He tends to act normally in front of others, so that nobody would believe it if you revealed what was going on between you.

He insists you cease contact with your family or friends.

If he drinks or takes mood-altering drugs, does his behaviour become more erratic and obnoxious?

Is it next to impossible to plan anything, such as a social engagement, because of his moodiness, impulsiveness or unpredictability? Do you find yourself having to make excuses for him?

If you've already encountered a man like this, you may be thinking, *"Wow, I had no idea that other people go through exactly the same thing as me."* Such a man may have borderline personality disorder (BPD). Threats to commit suicide are sometimes carried out. Their extreme fears of abandonment may stem from childhood trauma, yet their irrational, intense behaviour often encourages the very rejection they fear the most. These personality disorders can be devastating for the sufferers. Being in a relationship with one can be so much worse.

players

A 'player' is on a mission to have sex with as many different women as possible. Players use women. A player doesn't care about what any woman thinks or feels. He doesn't plan to see her again anyway. He's always more interested in the girl called 'next'. Rarely would a player physically harm a woman, but if she's hurt emotionally, as far as he's concerned, that's her problem. There is no emotional attachment with his 'conquests'. His only mission is to get laid. In order to achieve this he is an expert at lying, cheating and deceiving. He will be extremely manipulative, misleading and, above all, appear to be charm personified. But it's all an act.

While not gay, in many cases players don't actually like women, even though they claim to. A player often won't have many, if any, female friends. He's often a lonely loner. Many are addicted to 'the chase'. The sex is his 'reward' for demonstrating such skill and expertise in deceiving yet another woman who was 'stupid enough' to fall for him.

To him, sleeping with women is a numbers game. The more women he initiates conversations with, the higher the odds are that he'll be sexually successful. He doesn't care if he gets dozens of *"noes"*, if it leads to some *"yeses"*. He actively targets the 'plain Jane' especially if he's a good-looking guy. She'll be flattered that he's interested in her. It increases the chances that he'll get the only thing he wants from her. He can be patient as he turns up the charm, sure that he'll soon have her precisely where he wants her - horizontal. Then, once he's got what he wants, she can forget about the next date. He will simply disappear. Leaving the girl feeling 'used' and conned.

It must also be added here that having sex with a player puts you at higher risk of catching a sexual infection from him. Because he may have had sex with a lot of different women, you are effectively sleeping with everyone else he's slept with, and everyone they have slept with.

how to spot a player

Take the following seemingly innocent conversation a player might have with a girl he's targetted. He might say, *"Just for fun, who is your favourite Hollywood actor?"* (He'll then assess why you are attracted to that particular actor. He wants to know if it's sexual). Then he might go on, *"Just suppose you were in a hotel lobby with some girlfriends and that guy actually came in. What would you do? What if he 'noticed' you? What if he invited you to join him in his hotel room for the night? Would you go?"* If you said *"No"* to such a question, he knows that if Mr Hollywood actor won't get anywhere with you, he has no chance. He won't waste any more of his time on you. He'll leave to find someone who would say *"Yes"*.

Players really don't care what women think of them. Those who are disinterested in him are merely a delay.

They have learned to cultivate an aura of energy around them, appearing full of life, vitality and confidence. They do not appear intimidated at all.

A player is brilliant at initially making eye-contact with his next victim, and assuring himself of a welcoming response before he approaches. He then devotes his time making the woman feel good about herself. He makes sure that his conversation is not about the mundane. He will intrigue her by saying or asking about stuff she has probably not been asked before.

He makes a woman feel as if she is the sexiest woman in the world. And they tend to pick on women who don't usually feel that way at all – because they make the easiest victims. He knows how to make a woman laugh. He pays attention. He notices things and communicates what he's noticed about a woman, in subtle ways. All the while trying to make her feel super-special. He approaches women everywhere, not just in bars and clubs (where he knows women can be more guarded).

In fact, he appears to possess all the qualities you'd look for in a guy. The only problem is he only intends to 'pass by' – never to stay.

Nice women invariably allow themselves to get tangled up with varying types of dangerous men because they ignore their feminine instinct and silence that alarm bell. If a 'new' guy seems too good to be true – he's possibly perfected this illusion over many encounters. Listen to your instinct. Check him out. In fact, ask him to show you some ID. A lot of guys even lie about their names.

online grooming

Predators (male or female) have the remarkable ability to detect vulnerability and emotional weakness. And to prey on it without conscience. 'Grooming' is when a predator prepares a potential victim for future physical or sexual abuse. They actively target the young. The anonymity of the online world is perfect for predators.

How can you tell if you are being 'groomed'? Even the experts agree that it can be extremely difficult to know for sure whether someone is only being friendly, or if they have a more sinister agenda. These predators know this and can be incredibly cunning and sophisticated in how they create completely false identities. They deliberately focus on appearing trustworthy, sometimes over a long period.

If you meet someone online who shows a high level of interest in you, it appeals to your ego. Someone with low self-esteem will appreciate the attention even more. It's part of the trap. Beware of any stranger or person you have not met who says or does anything to make you feel 'special' or dependent on them for affection and attention. These are some of the telltale signs of someone 'grooming' you that you need to be on the lookout for. They:

- always appear to be online
- 'innocently' ask you repeatedly for personal information, supposedly so they can send you gifts
- want to know if you're lonely or depressed
- ask you questions of an intimate or sexual nature
- are keen to communicate with you at strange times of the day or night
- want to meet you alone
- want you to keep **any** secrets
- make you feel sorry for them
- appear 'too good to be true'.

Just one or two of these behaviours isn't enough to confirm for sure that you're being groomed. However, if you sense something is not quite right about somebody, even if you can't quite put your finger on why you have your suspicions, the best advice is to **trust your instinct**. Never agree to meet such an individual in person, even with a friend.

Dear Daughter
Being independent is great. However, it's NEVER smart to go anywhere, when no one else knows where you are.

what I wish I'd known about:

Marriage & divorce

"We think we're mature when we're graduating from high school, and we are so wrong! You change so much during college and in your first years in the workplace. You want to find a life partner who is a good match to that more mature, more self-aware person, not a partner to the immature you who may or may not grow in the same direction that you do. My daughter did follow my advice and is now married to a wonderful man who comple-ments her in a way that her high school and col-lege boyfriends never would have." Juli Klie

Decisions can be difficult at the best of times. Choos-ing the partner to marry is one of the most important choices you will ever make.

Full disclosure: I have been married and divorced twice. So you might be forgiven for thinking that I'm anti-marriage. Not at all. I'm anti-**bad** marriages. If this chap-ter stops just one bad marriage from happening, it has to be worth it: for women, men, as well as any children who come along as a result of such marriages. In the interest of simplicity, the term 'marriage' is used throughout this chapter, but please recognise that it applies equally to other types of long-term relationships, too.

what is marriage anyway?

Marriage is mostly about the friendship, love and com-mitment between two people sharing all aspects of day-to-day living: cooking, cleaning, ironing, and all the other tasks that go into running a household. Making joint decisions about where to live, what job to take (and what to do if you lose yours, or he loses his), what your priorities are and how to pay for them. Deciding on how large, or small, a family you want, when you want to start it, and how you wish to raise your children. And all of these decisions involve another person whose points of view will not always match yours.

Living together without getting married has become the preferred option for many couples. In Scandinavia, for example, it is widely recognised that the institution of marriage is dying. The link between marriage and parenthood has also been broken. A growing number of children are born out of wedlock without social stigma. However, living together still entails the same type of psychological and emotional commitment, and compromise, as a marriage. So even if you don't plan to marry, this chapter still includes important information for you.

The same holds true for same-sex marriages or partnerships: you are committing to another person, and that involves compromise. In most (but not all) cases, same-sex marriages don't include children (although this is becoming more common), but other legal responsibilities associated with straight marriages also apply.

what is a marriage . . . legally?

Being a loving couple, having children and living happily ever after is the goal of most men and women when they get married. Marriage used to be a 'holy union in the eyes of God.' Although this belief is still upheld by many, legally the government now runs the marriage 'franchise'. The Church no longer has the same power it used to have.

When you sign a marriage license you accept the terms of your government. It is a legally binding 'business' contract. Most of the contract terms are irrelevant if you stay married. However, if you divorce, how assets are split can have a monumental impact on your life and your future options. Although the details vary by country, the main clauses are fairly uniform. For example, when you get married all assets are shared equally. A farmer once commented following his marriage, *"I remember walking up the aisle owning a farm, and walking back down the aisle owning half a farm."* Debts, regardless of who incurs them, are shared equally. If you marry someone with undisclosed debts, you are still liable for them.

Marry the right man and both of your lives will be enriched beyond your wildest dreams. Marry the wrong man and you face the distinct possibility that you will endure a living nightmare. Ask any woman who has been divorced to tell you what it was like. Even the best divorces are emotionally draining. You really don't want to know about the worst.

caught in the crossfire of a parents' divorce

When parents divorce, life can get difficult for the children too, regardless of their age. Confusion and loneliness is commonplace. Some children convince themself that it was somehow their 'fault'. In other cases, parents expect each child to be more loyal to them, than to the other parent. Some even encourage their children to hate the other parent.

Divorces occur for a variety of complex reasons. And parents don't always deal with divorce as well as they might. They do the best they can of course, but sometimes children suffer in ways they really should not be subjected to. Let's take one common scenario: one parent has an affair. The other parent feels utterly distraught, betrayed and deeply angry. In some cases, the 'victim' parent feels the need to retaliate by finding a way to hurt the parent who had the affair. Knowing how much that parent loves their children, they then set about turning those children against that parent as a way of 'punishing' the cheating husband or wife. It's called Parental Alienation Syndrome (PAS for short).

Unfortunately, it is also a form of child abuse. But the angry parent, so wrapped up in their own intense emotional pain, rarely sees it that way.

If, during a divorce, either your mother or your father tries to turn you against the other parent, it's really important not to allow yourself to get sucked into it. Any parent who tries to do so needs to be told, *"I love you both. I won't allow myself to take sides."* This stance can also be extremely helpful for younger brothers and sisters to witness. It will give them the courage to do the same.

Divorce rips lives apart. Whether or not you experienced it as a child, it clearly is something you want to avoid as an adult. Of course, one way is to not get married in the first place. However, whilst there are people who make the choice to live with a partner and never marry, for the majority of us this is still not the standard option.

So what can you do, if anything, to choose your future husband wisely? You might find it helpful to understand the various different reasons men and women get married.

why some men marry

Generalisations are never accurate. Even so, here are a few reasons men have given for deciding to get married (we'll get to women in a moment). As you will see, not all of them are great reasons.

love

Firstly, there's love. Both are so deeply in love. They were made for each other, true soul mates and best friends. They know each other incredibly well, they have mutual respect for each other and genuinely want the same from life. They have found lasting happiness and will remain together for the rest of their long lives. That's the plan, at least. And many times it works. But not always.

falling into it

He loves his girlfriend. Maybe they've been together for a long time. Pressure from families: *"So when are you two going to tie the knot?"* Or, she may be so keen to get married, many men become GAGs – Go Along Guys. A man like this will propose to show how committed he is to the relationship.

Perhaps she has discovered she's pregnant, so he proposes in a gesture to make an 'honest woman' of her.

He may think that he's starting to feel a little too old for the singles bars he has frequented for a number of years – another sign that it is time for that next phase of his life.

If his male friends are starting to get married, he may think he had better do it, too. If not, he could be left on his own.

When a man starts to lose his hair, he often sees it as the first sign that he'd better think about settling down before he becomes too unappealing to women. If the hair loss coincides with packing on a bit of weight, his fear of being left on his own sharpens his mind further.

How old he feels and how old others make him feel will also have an impact on his openness to the idea of marriage.

Perhaps she wants to marry him, so she proposes. He is grateful or flattered that someone wants him and he agrees.

In some cases he is incredibly needy, neurotic and his Emotional Core is weak. He starts to feel desperate for a wife. His interactions with his girlfriend start to to take on the tone of a sales pitch as he tries to convince her.

If your boyfriend has made it clear to you that he would happily get married, you must find out why it appeals to him, and what he sees as your role as his future wife.

why some women marry

Just as we did with the men, let's look at some of the reasons women decide to marry. It's important to realise how so many young girls are brought up to view marriage. Millions of kind, loving and well-meaning parents tuck their little girls up in bed at night and feed them a diet of fairy stories featuring beautiful young girls who meet handsome princes, fall in love, marry and live happily ever after.

Some parents put stickers on their cars proclaiming to the world: *'Little Princess On Board'*. How might these parents unwittingly create unrealistic expectations about what marriage is and the role of men as future husbands? And how many of these innocent little girls start to believe they are princesses? And how many learn, subconsciously perhaps, to expect to be treated like royalty by everyone, especially men – because that's what daddy did? Does any of this describe your friends? Or even you?

Some women seem to be in love with the ideal of what marriage 'should' be, and the notion of having a party in their honour on a day when they will be the centre of attention, looking beautiful. Marriage is therefore an aspiration for some women from a young age. Unfortunately, many of these women dream of a wedding, not a marriage.

Other women want the status of being a 'wife'. In her mind, it validates her as a woman. She likes being described as someone's wife. Not being 'chosen' as a wife could be regarded by her as being a failure as a woman.

Still, others are lonely and see their future husband's role as someone who will 'make her happy'. When he fails, as he usually does, she may blame him.

Most people are genetically programmed to want children, but the tendency seems to be stronger at an earlier age in women than in men. Some women are more determined than others, especially if they reach an age when their girlfriends are marrying in droves. A woman may start to feel that if she doesn't find a man soon, it might be too late to have children. Women from their late twenties and into their mid-thirties become increasingly aware of how loud their biological baby clock is ticking.

You may have other reasons for wanting to get married. Be clear in your mind about what you think to be your role as a wife, and what you feel the husband's role is. What are your motivations and expectations? If you already have a fiancé, find out exactly what he feels about all this, too. Your roles are equally important.

before you marry: mate selection

Be open-minded and learn to be non-judgmental. Good looks and cool posing might appeal right now, but it's so much easier being married to a man who makes you laugh, and is kind to you. One who is there for you, and let's you know it. Who knows, that guy who is two inches 'too short' may turn out to be the most wonderful man for you in the long run.

Dear Daughter
The types of men you date today will most likely end up being nothing at all like the man you one day marry.

Don't ever enter a marriage thinking that you are going to be able to change the man you love into someone even 'better'. Believing that he would be prepared to change 'if he loved you', isn't going to make any difference either. If you truly love your man, you will accept him warts and all, and vice versa.

But what can you do to improve the chances that you don't choose the wrong guy to marry? This isn't foolproof, but you need to conduct 'due diligence'.

due diligence

Here are some sobering facts. Just over 50% of all marriages end in divorce. And about 40% of second marriages also fail.

After reading all this, should you be pessimistic about marriage? Absolutely not. But you need to be realistic. Too many people still go into marriage with their eyes closed. They are not aware of what they are getting into.

In our book, *That Bitch*, my co-author Mary T Cleary and I created a document called a '*Due Diligence Checklist*'. It is equally useful for men and women, and lists many questions to ask each other to uncover any information that either party needs to know before going ahead with a marriage. It deals with attitudes towards life, including roles and responsibilities. Numerous married people told us that they wish they'd had those conversations before they got married.

You can download this checklist for free from www. TheSensibleUncle.com/DD. For anyone who is planning to get married, do them a favour and send this link to them.

how you disagree

Conflict and confrontation are natural parts of life. Some people thrive on creating it, while others will agree to almost anything in order to avoid it. Which type are you? Which type is he? If one of you were described as a bit 'bossy', which of you might they be talking about?

Some young couples are proud of the fact that they don't argue. This is not necessarily a good sign. It may be because you are 'in synch'. But it may be because one of you chooses not to argue. Swallowing anger or resentment does not make it go away, either on your part or his. Eventually it comes out.

In addition, you must understand how he fights. Is he reasonable, calm, and empathetic? How often is he unreasonable? How often does he have childish tantrums and sulks? Is he prone to making demands that only take his interests into account? Does he always insist on getting his own way? If so, do you give in for an 'easier life'? Or is it the other way around?

Each time anyone avoids confrontation by giving in for an 'easier life', it reinforces the other person's expectation of getting their own way in the future. This is not healthy for any relationship. Give and take is good – but never if it's predominantly one person who does the giving and the other who does the taking.

Being married to a man who has learned to expect to get whatever he wants most, if not all, of the time, could come back to haunt you.

Also consider how he responds when you treat him well. Does he express warm appreciation of such behaviour, or does he just seem to naturally expect it, or does he actually demand it? And how does that make you feel?

What about your attitude towards him? Do you appreciate, expect or demand particular behaviours of him? Have you ever noticed his reaction? Pay attention. Other attitudes you need to pay attention to:

- How self-obsessed is he?
- Is he kind or cruel to people?
- How does he behave when no one is watching?
- What do your friends really think about him? Ask them seriously. Observe the delay before they say anything. That could tell you a lot.
- Are relatively small things always blown up into full-scale dramas by him?
- Does he see conflict as a battle that he must always win? If so, being married to him could get ugly one day.

For some men or women, early in a relationship it can appear quite appealing that their partner tends to make most of the decisions. So long as both parties are happy with this it can work well for a long time. It is not uncommon, however, for those attitudes to change, sometimes quite abruptly, and for the relationship to suddenly collapse.

Just suppose, your boyfriend sees you as a strong decisive type and is happy for you to make a lot of the decisions. He sees it as a sign that you care about him. But what if, as he gets older, he grows in confidence and starts to resent the fact that you make all the decisions? His resentment could become a belief that you are being too 'controlling'. Although to you, you're just doing what you have always done. It happens the other way around too. Indeed, this is often cited as one of the most common reasons why women file for divorce.

pre-nuptial agreements

If a man dares to suggest to his future wife that they sign a pre-nuptial agreement he risks an accusation of being unromantic and distrustful. But pre-nuptial agreements make enormous sense for men or women who own substantially more assets or cash than their partner before marriage. Pre-nups, as they are called, would state that both parties retain full ownership of pre-marriage assets or cash if the marriage ends in divorce. Pre-nups are not always recognised by the courts, although they are being accepted far more widely than in the past.

If your future husband is rich and he, or his family, requests or demands that you sign a pre-nup, it is essential that you obtain independent legal advice (not from his lawyer). Likewise, if you are rich, and he isn't, he needs to get independent legal advice.

This issue is controversial. The purpose for including it here is merely to illustrate how seriously you need to consider what you are buying into when you decide to marry.

how to make a marriage work

Happy marriages are based on a deep, mutually respectful friendship. They involve two people who really like each other. They always remember to greet their partner with warmth and enthusiasm, regardless of what sort of day they've had. They know that taking grumpiness out on an innocent partner is unkind and never justified.

Happy marriages don't happen by accident. They require equal energy and commitment from both parties. It's never the job of your partner to make you happy or to 'complete you'. Each party needs to be equally committed to making their partner feel secure in the relationship. In such an environment, privacy is also respected at all times.

Attitudes to money, sex and family are in alignment (and mutually agreed before they marry).

Happily married couples always keep their own identities, yet they openly talk and think in terms of 'us' and 'we'. Children are 'ours', never 'mine'. Couples say 'please' and 'thank you' to each other even after many years together. They don't take each other for granted – ever.

Regardless of daily pressures, happy couples ring-fence quality 'date' time every week. They take time to nourish their relationship and often share some (but not all) interests. These fun, intimate moments create a bank of shared loving memories, which in turn strengthens their relationship.

Happy couples don't keep score. Being happy together is more important to happy couples than insisting on being 'right' all the time.

Differences are accepted. They add richness to a relationship. One partner doesn't try to change the other. However, if someone knows that a particular habit causes the other to get upset, in a respectful relationship, the 'offending' partner will attempt to improve their behaviour. And the other partner will acknowledge those attempts.

Life often throws challenges and difficulties at a relationship. Happy couples face them together. They know that they are stronger together. And they resolve to work together to overcome them.

Romantic love and passionate love over time get replaced by a deeper form of love for one another. Happy couples decide to love (and stay in love with) each other. Is all of this difficult? Yes. But when you're married to the right person it's so worth it.

Long-term love and friendship is based on warmth. Not on how 'hot' either of you are.

So choose your husband well. And don't be in too much of a hurry to do so.

what I wish I'd known about:

sex

For religious, cultural or other reasons you may have decided not to engage in sex outside marriage, or to have any form of casual sex. If you are sure you will stick to this view, feel free to skip this section.

For the rest of you, this chapter covers what is almost always omitted from formal sex education lessons. You're probably already so tired of hearing about the mechanics of sex: the 'what fits where' stuff and hearing 'always insist he uses a condom', 'irresponsible sex gives you diseases' and 'don't get pregnant'. As well-meaning (and as critically important and true) as that information is, it doesn't necessarily help you to know what to do when you finally find yourself with a guy, perhaps for the first time.

This chapter is deliberately written in a direct, no-nonsense way. Some readers (especially curious parents) may find it unsettling. It's not intended to shock, but deals with the sexual realities experienced by so many young men and women today. By cutting through the myths, the guilt and morality issues and a great deal of confusion, it is hoped that you will gain a more balanced, less prejudiced view of sex and the part it will play in your future life.

Sex is supposed to be pleasurable; if it wasn't, humans wouldn't do it and we'd die out as a species. The question is: how much of a slave are you to pleasure?

how NOT to learn about sex

According to research, a substantial proportion of boys and girls all over the world now think they learn about sex by watching porn on the Internet. If this describes you, please, please erase what you believe sex is all about based on what you may have seen.

Watching a man banging away at a submissive woman who is being paid to look and sound like she's enjoying it, is **not** what real sex is about. Nor are such images helpful to you or any man you will ever have sex with.

Pornography is a hugely profitable global business. It is only interested in making money. Free porn is offered purely to persuade (mostly) men to pay for it. Do not confuse porn with sex. Or confuse sex with love-making. Porn is not sex education either. And that includes a lot of so-called sex education DVDs.

Most porn only focuses on male sexual self-gratification. In those cases it completely ignores the female perspective. For a sexually inexperienced woman who has viewed Internet porn, she may be led to believe that this is what is expected of her. This is absolutely **not** the case. Porn is a completely false representation of what to do and feel. Hardcore porn movies include sexual acts that are not normal. For example, normal sex is never ever violent, nor does it involve anything that is physically painful or degrading to a woman.

And any man who thinks that sex is purely for his own pleasure (as a lot of self-obsessed men do), and an opportunity to star in his own version of the porn movies he's watched, is not someone you are advised to have sex with. These types of men don't really care who agrees to have sex with them – all they want is someone to say *"yes"* and, as crass as it sounds, for that woman to provide him with localised friction for his penis or his fingers. If that means plying a woman with drink or drugs to get what he wants, he'll do it. These men really don't care about you, or how you feel during or after your sexual encounter with him.

Men who view a lot of Internet porn tend to get fixated

on the idea of 'doing it'. And think in terms of 'doing you'. They don't necessarily think of a sexual partner as a person in her own right, but as an object to be used and abused.

Most importantly, don't be fooled into what's 'normal' yourself. For example, all girls are not shaved all over, so don't be pressured into copying such trends.

sex and chocolate

Sex is a bit like chocolate. Cheap, poor quality chocolate can taste OK if there's nothing else available, but only when you've tasted and slowly savoured the best chocolate, lovingly made by a world-class chocolatier, can you really appreciate the vast differences.

Many of us have gorged ourselves on cheap chocolate. At the time it may satisfy a craving, but later, regret and self-loathing often creeps in. It's also a bit like that with sex sometimes.

Devouring a lot of chocolate feeds the cravings of the hungry ghost as described on page 21. Sexual cravings are sometimes driven by the hungry ghost too. Sex promises short-term feelings of intimacy or a sense of feeling 'wanted'. But it's often an unsatisfying illusion, especially with a casual partner.

Women with low self-esteem routinely 'trade' their deeper emotional needs for relatively brief moments of sexual ecstasy which become a temporary escape from poor feelings about themselves. Those with even bigger self-esteem issues also tend to 'self-medicate' to dull the 'pain' with booze or drugs, before they embark on their next 'fun-filled', casual sexual encounter. And when that doesn't make them feel good about themselves, there's always the next person and the next, etc. In fact, many women, naturally desiring a 'proper' relationship, mistakenly think that getting to sex quickly will jump-start love. When it doesn't, feelings of rejection can intensify the urge for love, which leads to more sex too soon, and a potentially destructive pattern of future behaviour.

Our earliest sexual experiences have a critically important effect on all future sexual relationships. You have a responsibility to yourself to make your early sexual experiences positive ones.

> *"When you come from an abused background as I did, you believe responsibility lies with those who have power over you. They use it to control you. I didn't know it was OK to take responsibility for myself. When boundaries have been broken through neglect or abuse in childhood, it's common to feel powerlessness. A way of regaining that power and responsibility in later life is to seek the help of a counsellor either through your doctor or privately."* Anonymous woman (46).

To develop a healthy long-term attitude towards your own sexuality and sexual appetites, let's look at some of what's on offer.

For many men and women, sex is nothing more than a contact sport. It's just another type of 'sweaty workout'. Who they do it with isn't that important because there's no shared emotional connection. Difficulties often arise when one of the participants becomes emotionally involved while the other does not. It's a myth that it's always the women who get involved romantically while men don't. It can happen to anyone.

At the other end of the scale, sex is the mutual expression of such deep love, intimacy and affection between two people that both parties may deliberately set out to conceive a baby through their lovemaking.

Between these two extremes is a wide range of sexual behaviour: masturbation; pornography; one-night stands; male and female prostitution; friends-with-benefits; orgies; threesomes; swingers and fetish parties; longer-term, casual, sexually based relationships; and committed longer-term relationships in which sex plays an important but non-dominant role.

With the right person, sex can be intensely physical, exciting, passionate and intoxicating. It releases natural hormones that can make you feel utterly amazing. Sex can also lead to a deep emotional, even spiritual, connection with your partner.

With the wrong partner, sex can still feel intensely pleasurable during the act itself, but afterwards there is often an emotional emptiness, a deep sense of regret, shame, guilt or a feeling of being used or even abused.

your sexual pleasure

Sexual pleasure is directly linked to your mindset and your motivations for having sex. This usually boils down to a simple fact: are you having sex to **take** pleasure, to **give** pleasure or to **share** pleasure?

sharing

Without doubt, the desire of both partners to share sexual pleasure is the basis for the most deeply satisfying sex life for any couple. This occurs when each person knows the other at a profoundly intimate level: each other's bodies, what gives the most sensuous physical pleasure, and how they are able to connect intellectually, emotionally and spiritually. A complex combination of touch, words, movements and, above all, consideration all come together to create this true intimacy. It's like two people devoted to learning complete fluency in a private language. All this takes time, patience, understanding and a true commitment to each other. Many couples, married for decades, don't reach this level of sexual intimacy. It certainly isn't going to happen if you've just met someone in a bar.

giving

This happens between people who know and care about each other up to a point; one gives pleasure, the other takes the pleasure. A healthy relationship means they take it in turns. In these cases, sex tends to be done **to** each other, rather than **with** each other. Being open to receiving pleasure is perfectly natural and nurtures one's healthy needs. A partner may gain pleasure by giving pleasure, but its unlikely to be truly fulfilling for both parties longer-term. When you find yourself always or mostly receiving sexual pleasure, it's a form of 'selfish sex'. If you are the one nearly always giving, you are open to feeling 'used'. With equal give and take, many relationships seem to function at this sexual level.

taking

And there's 'casual'; the 'ultra-selfish' type of sex. This is when two relative strangers get together to take as much as they can from each other to satisfy their own personal sexual desires. Driven by lust, it can be intense, even addictive and satisfies short-term cravings with a 'fix' from our pleasure hormones; the equivalent of cheap chocolate sex.

Give, take or share; there's nothing inherently right or wrong about having sex with a consenting adult. What is important though is understanding your sexual motivators. Oppressed during childhood, do you feel the need to rebel against your parents, or a religious upbringing? Are you determined to live your life on the edge, free of any control either from them or yourself? The prospect of others disapproving of you, being a 'bad girl', exerting sexual power over guys, can all be incredibly appealing.

Not only are there different types of sexual relationship, it's also about which ones you are most drawn to.

Why? And what you are prepared to 'pay' for your sexual freedom. After all, everything has a price. And longer-term consequences. It's so much easier not to think about them. And is why a lot of people don't. It's easy to be easy. Knowing when to say *"no"*, when you'd rather say *"yes"* can be quite a challenge when everyone around you claims to be 'doing it' all the time.

self-love

Before we explore sex with a partner, masturbation plays a role in the lives of many young men and women. It's perfectly natural. It can help you relax, can be comforting, helping you to get to sleep and let off the 'steam' associated with normal sexual frustration. And you can do it solely for your own personal pleasure without taking into consideration the needs or desires of a partner.

It is also safe because you don't catch STDs from yourself. Discovering how to give yourself sexual pleasure is part of growing up. Stroke, caress and explore your body. Learn how to arouse yourself. If you want to, use sex toys (your own; there are some things you don't share with friends). Get to know your own body intimately. Know what you like and what you don't. When you are at your most relaxed, you are more likely (but never guaranteed) to reach orgasm through masturbation, rather than sexual intercourse. Remember to lock your door first so you aren't disturbed or interrupted.

your 'sacred' home

Sexual intercourse obviously involves a man entering your body. Think of your body as a 'sacred home'. For women with a strong Emotional Core, they treat it as a very special place. What you think or believe about your body is directly linked to who you are prepared to invite 'inside' and how often. Realise that most men want as many such invitations as possible. And some are not that bothered where those invitations come from. Who in their right mind would keep their home clean and tidy only to allow a stream of people with muddy boots to march through it? And a lot of men then want to tell as many people as possible where they've been and with whom. You have a duty to yourself to only invite those who are prepared to respect your sacred home.

OK and not OK

It's OK and natural for you to want to have sex. And to enjoy it. It's OK to have as many different sexual partners as you want. (The various reasons why you might want to are discussed elsewhere in this chapter.) It's OK to be curious and to experiment with as many forms of sexual pleasure as you see fit. It is your life. And your body.

It's also OK for you to say *"no"* to sex at any time, even if or when you are in a longer-term sexual relationship with someone special. And it's OK to refuse to take part in any sexual behaviour you feel uncomfortable about. If your instinct tells you something is weird, it probably is. At least for now. If you refuse a partner (especially someone you may not actually know that well), it's OK for him to feel disappointed, but it's not OK for him to get irritated, annoyed or angry with you. Or to put you under any form of pressure to do what he wants. If, for example, he wants you to perform oral sex on him and you don't want to, don't be pressured into it. Implied or explicit threats by him are never OK. Any pressure, should be taken as a warning that he is not interested in your well-being. It is also OK for you to require him to wear a condom. Adopt the mantra *"No glove. No love. No exceptions"*. It is absolutely not OK for him to try to persuade you to allow him to have unprotected sex with you for whatever reason or excuse he might give you. If he says it spoils his enjoyment, that's tough for him. Be confident about this. It's always OK for you to insist he uses a condom. End of subject.

It is not OK for you to agree to sex when you are not ready for it. And it is never OK for you to agree to sex as a way of getting someone to 'like' you more.

"Women need a reason to have sex. Men just need a place." Billy Crystal, comedian.

teenage pregnancy

Despite a small drop in recent years, the UK still has the dubious honour of having the highest rates of teenage pregnancy in Europe. It's widely accepted that most young girls unintentionally get pregnant despite extensive sex education and contraception advice. Some girls bow to pressure from boyfriends to have unprotected sex, but in some cases getting pregnant is a deliberate act. Teenage pregnancy can even be 'contagious' according to a Norwegian study, where it found that teenage girls are more likely to get pregnant if they have an older sister who also had a baby as a teenager.

In the minds of some girls, especially those from unhappy and/or abusive families, pregnancy is seen as an escape; they believe they'll get free housing, financial support from their government and a baby who will provide the unconditional love they never received as children themselves. As they later discover, this rarely, if ever happens.

the first time

The single most common regret I've heard from women about the first time they had sex was being drunk. They thought it would calm their nerves, but, with hindsight, they wished they'd remained sober. So stay sober. Nervousness is normal. Feeling scared could be a sign that you are not ready, or you are with the wrong guy.

"Will it hurt?" is a common question. Women agree that it can be a little bit painful, or slightly uncomfortable the first time. However, this is almost always as a consequence of the following: an overly impatient man who isn't prepared to help his partner to relax and who puts the woman under pressure to have sex before she is fully aroused and physically ready for him to enter her. A woman's body is designed to accommodate a man during sex. Having sex before natural lubrication has been produced can lead to uncomfortable or painful sex for the woman. But when a young woman is fully aroused, she will naturally produce enough lubrication around and inside her vagina and be far more likely to experience pleasure rather than any pain.

It doesn't help when girlfriends who claim to have 'done it' make it sound scary. If they do have this sexual experience, it is highly probable that they weren't relaxed, they felt rushed by the guy and weren't truly ready when it happened.

As he pushes himself fully inside you for the first time, you may experience a sensation of something like the stretching (and pushing through) of an elastic band inside you, as your hymen is broken. This is perfectly natural if it happens. If that doesn't happen, that's natural too.

If you have concerns about having sex for the first time, why not sit down with your boyfriend and read this chapter together and then talk about it? Even if your boyfriend has little or no sexual experience himself, if he isn't interested in talking to you about your feelings at this important time in your life – don't do it with him.

Your biggest challenge is probably slowing him down. If he's like most inexperienced guys he'll be solely focused on 'the main event'. This is where men and women are so different. As a woman, you want to slowly savour every touch, to feel delicious, sensuous pleasure ripple throughout your entire body before you invite him inside. Many guys don't understand that. They just want to 'do it'!

Inexperienced (and sexually frustrated) men have to contend with a potentially embarrassing condition called premature ejaculation. Guys can get so excited, so quickly that they will 'come' far, far sooner than they (or you) would want them to. However, young guys recover quickly and are often set to go again fairly soon afterwards. So the longer he has to wait, the higher the likelihood he'll ejaculate prematurely. In a way, it's actually a compliment to you – you are turning him on too much.

Unfortunately, a men can get so wrapped up in trying to impress with his energy and even his acrobatic skills, he ignores how the girl is feeling. Staying power is a skill he has yet to master – and it's all over fast. He collapses on top of her with a huge grin on his face thinking he's the Master of the Universe, while she's feeling terribly let down, thinking, *"OMG, was that it? When is he going to get off me?"*

If your partner is someone you know well, (which is always the preferred option in the early days of sexual activity because you can both learn together), gently slow him down. If he persists out of sheer frustration, ask or tell him to stop whatever he's doing. Take his hand(s) and place them where ever you want to be touched. Ahead of time, tell him that you'll let him know when you're ready. And only go ahead when/if you are.

what turns men on

The short answer is – just about anything. It's been joked that to turn on a man all a woman needs is a pulse. Or for her to show up naked with a six-pack of beer.

Seriously though, normal male sexuality is fairly straightforward. In the vast majority of cases, men are stimulated visually. Seeing a real semi-naked woman or pictures of one will often be enough to arouse him. And just about everything else centres almost exclusively around what he has between his legs, his penis and testicles. Any attention by a woman in that area will turn him on. A few words of warning though: a man's testicles are extremely sensitive. If you choose to touch them, stroke, never squeeze them. Squeezing his balls can be excruciatingly painful to him. By contrast, when you touch a penis, you can be far rougher than you might think. Pulling and squeezing his penis can be highly pleasurable for a man. However, pulling his foreskin back (if he has one) towards his body too hard can be painful. So, that's all you need to know? Not really.

Unlike girls, a lot of boys and young guys are not brought up experiencing 'touch'. Men are generally not used to being touched at all. But behind the bravado and 'tough-guy' pretend image portrayed by a lot of men is someone who likes to be cuddled, to feel close, to feel the warmth of another person – at least some of the time. In the same way that you may like to have someone run their fingers through your hair, or stroke your back, tummy, legs and thighs, or have your ears and neck kissed gently, so do men (although a lot may not yet realise it). For a man to receive a non-sexual massage from a woman will make him feel very special (even though he may initially find it difficult to relax, or fear that he'll get aroused at a time when he thinks he shouldn't).

If you were to ask the average young guy what he liked or how he'd like to be touched (other than 'there'), he probably wouldn't even know.

Real intimacy can be achieved between two people through mutual non-sexual touching. It is a vastly underrated activity. Learn how to give a non-sexual massage. It is a highly regarded life-skill. Anyone who receives a massage by someone who knows what they are doing will be so appreciative. There are lots of books and courses where you can learn these techniques. Practise with your girlfriends. It's not a sexual thing.

But with a lover, it you want it to, a non-sexual massage can also easily evolve into a deeply sensuous shared experience.

are you any good in bed?

Far too many young women worry unduly about whether they are any 'good' at sex. It's the wrong way of thinking about it. It's not a test. Or a competition.

That said, most sexually experienced men agree that women can be too passive in bed. This could be for a variety of reasons. Perhaps she is so immersed in her own pleasure that she fails to think of what he might want from her. Or maybe she doesn't know how to be proactive. It could even be she's afraid that he'll think she's too keen or too experienced. This is especially true in a new sexual relationship. She doesn't necessarily want him to think she's learned all that stuff by sleeping with a lot of men.

The easiest way to really turn on a guy is to be more proactive. Particularly if you are in a long-term relationship with one person. Take the initiative at times. Learn what he really likes. And so long as you are happy doing what he likes, he will appreciate your attention.

Most importantly, have fun. Laugh together. But please don't point at parts of him and laugh at the same time!

Like any woman, he also wants to feel 'wanted' sexually. For any man to feel that his girlfriend is really into him, is a huge compliment to him. If his girlfriend occasionally takes over and 'takes advantage of him' sexually (with his permission of course), she will drive him wild. And he will probably adore her for that.

enjoy being a turned on woman

A horny man can have a full erection in less than five seconds. He's ready. Women are never ever that quick. If it takes you a long time to feel fully aroused, you are normal. There is nothing wrong with your body. Never worry about not getting turned on 'quickly enough' or reaching orgasm within a certain time. Trying to have an orgasm is a sure way to ensure you won't be able to. Conscious of not getting to the 'finishing post' or not even feeling you're nearly there delays it even more, and before you know it you're in a vicious cycle, unable to reach orgasm. Many women never achieve orgasm. If you are one of those women, there's nothing wrong with you. Orgasm through sexual intercourse is also elusive for a lot of women.

Men like the idea that their sexual prowess is so finely honed that they can trigger orgasms for their lover. Never fake an orgasm 'for him'. The sad reality is that women who get into the habit of doing this are actually cheating themselves out of these wondrous feelings in the future. It teaches the body to behave in this way the next time and the next until it can become a psychological problem in itself.

Women often spoil their own sexual experience by being too self-conscious about her body. Being shy is natural, but worrying about what he thinks about your body before, during and after sex is guaranteed to detract from your enjoyment. Please don't do this. Almost all men are so preoccupied, they really don't think about it. Nor is it wise to worry about what he thinks or wants. This isn't to suggest you should be selfish, but your top priority is to fully relax physically and mentally and give yourself permission to truly enjoy yourself. Do that and an attentive partner will have a much better time, too.

the afterglow

After all the excitement, it's finally over. You are both lying there thoroughly exhausted and hopefully equally satisfied. Then what? The biggest gripe a lot of women have about men after sex is that all they want to do is roll over and fall asleep. (Or if it's a one-night stand, he probably can't wait to get out of the door. This is the part of casual sex that can result in you feeling really bad about yourself afterwards.) Either way, this is **not** the time to even think about starting a conversation with your guy. A 'heavy' or complicated discussion is an absolute no-no. He will almost certainly be incapable of doing so. Really. He may even resent you for trying. Even 'good' men can't help it.

I hope this chapter has given you a lot to think about, whether you are sexually experienced or not. It is a huge subject and plays a significant role in the lives of men and women of all ages, although as you get older in a stable long-term relationship, sex becomes less of the physical contact sport variety, and more an expression of deep affection and intimacy between two people who love and care about each other.

And they may have ditched the cheap chocolate years ago.

what I wish I'd known about:

work

> *"Some women choose to follow men, and some women choose to follow their dreams. If you're wondering which way to go, remember that your career will never wake up and tell you that it doesn't love you anymore."* Lady Gaga, singer.

Elliott is twenty. His story is equally relevant to all young women.

> *"When I was sixteen, my dad kept telling me that I should get a Saturday job. I didn't want to listen. He'd introduced me to a guy who seemed to like me. He was the manager of a local computer shop. Eventually my dad persuaded me to go to my first job interview. I was rubbish. Looking back I had no idea. I wouldn't have given **me** the job! But I got it anyway.*
>
> *"I helped customers with their problems, got things to work for them and sometimes mended stuff. It forced me to talk to people. I felt really awkward at first but pushed myself. It was a pain to have to get up every Saturday so early, but after a while I got used to it. Not only that, after about six months the manager called me into his office. I was petrified. He sat me down and offered me a pay rise! I hadn't even asked. He told me how impressed he'd been with the way I dealt with customers.*
>
> *"He valued knowing that I always showed up for work on time. And he really appreciated it if there was a problem I knew I couldn't handle, I'd*

ask him for help. That job really helped me.

"Quite recently I had a three week work place-ment at a company as part of my college course. One day a guy my age had to 'shadow' me. Even though I tried to get him to ask me questions, he didn't say a word. All he did was sit there using his hand to prop up his head on the desk. He was totally uninterested. He just didn't 'get it'. In that moment I realised how much I'd learned from my first job. I didn't want to believe it at the time but learning the discipline of working was the abso-lute best advice I could have had from my dad.

"I have a lot to thank him for."

There is always work that needs to be done. And there are people who are prepared to pay good money for the right person to do that work. If you want to be that right person, this chapter will help you.

The unemployment rate among young people runs at up to 50% in some countries. It's very tough in the job market. Working for a university degree has come with a very high price: massive levels of tuition debt and the realisation that these new degrees may or may not be relevant to potential future employers.

Companies are just not hiring like they used to. So there are far fewer jobs available, especially starting po-sitions. Stories of graduates applying for jobs and never even getting replies – never mind jobs – are now com-monplace. And those who are lucky enough to get a job interview then get told that they are competing with hundreds of other applicants, many of whom are equally overqualified for whatever jobs are available. It can be really tough and demoralising out there. There's very lit-tle chance that things will get easier any time soon.

Janet is a highly experienced career counsellor. She shared these insights:

"I see a lot of young single mothers in their late teens and early twenties. They are trying to live on benefit and are struggling financially. They have come to realise they absolutely have to find a job in order to make ends meet. But they face real problems; being single parents they need flexible hours but there are so few jobs offering that. And those jobs that do are usually poorly paid. By the time these women have paid for childcare whilst they are at work, in many cases there is so little left over that it's barely worth their while financially to go to work in the first place. It's a very cruel trap.

"How to get a first job (any job) requires being flexible, creative and proactive. Being willing to try anything, to offer filling in at a moment's notice if someone goes sick, doing some voluntary work just to get a foot in the door, or offering to work unsocial hours (if it's legal for their age), is going to make them stand out from the hundreds of others who want the same job.

"It's so important to get used to a work mindset. It can easily start in the home: taking responsibility for part of the running of the home at an early age, clearing up after a meal, teaching parents how to use their computer or tidying their own bedroom (that comment never seems to go down well!).

"These types of activity strengthen an ability to be responsible and reliable. It also gives them confidence that they can do something well and a feeling of being part of a team. And if they play their cards right they may get a bit of extra pocket money too.

"A lot of the university-educated young people do not have enough relevant work experience, no connections in their industry/profession and *if they haven't worked throughout their studies they can often have a very unrealistic idea about the work environment. Unfortunately, many have had depression and other health problems that have affected their careers."*

Decide today that you are a business. It's your time, your knowledge, or your interpersonal skills that customers and clients pay for, if you know how to sell yourself to them. Even if there seem to be no jobs, you can still find meaningful work. The next few pages will show you how. And in the process, will arm you with real skills that employers or clients are prepared to pay you for.

Let's start with some thoughts on what too many people don't understand about the world of work. By understanding this stuff, you'll put yourself at an advantage.

Firstly, you must decide to be worth more to your employer than they are actually paying you. You don't just do what you think you need to do for the money you are being paid. You need to do far more. It's absolutely essential that you are perceived as someone who really cares about delivering as much value as possible to the person or organisation that you are working for. If you aren't prepared to develop this mindset, don't be surprised if employers or clients refuse to take you on, let you go, or look for someone to replace you the next time they need work done.

Caring about what your client, customer or employer wants to achieve is incredibly important. And you need to take on at least some of the responsibility for helping them achieve the result they're looking for.

This mindset or attitude towards work is probably the most important thing for you to realise.

Don't fall into the trap of being told by colleagues with a bad attitude what you can get away with. Learning a bad attitude will cost you in the longer run.

Joe is now a dad in his fifties. He vividly remembers his start in the job market:

>"*My first job was when I was about fifteen, helping out in a local shop on weekends. Fortunately the owner was a family friend, because he took the time to quickly put a stop to what could have become a permanent bad attitude. One of my jobs was to sweep and mop up the floor at the end of the day. I was usually tired by then, and lazily swept and swabbed.*
>
>"*After a few days of this he stopped me, took the broom and, forcefully taking long sweeps, said, 'This is how you sweep. With energy and purpose. Because if you can sweep with energy at the end of a hard day you can do anything with energy, and any boss you ever have will notice it. Never just go through the motions of a job, no matter how menial. Really do it. There will be time to rest when you get home.'*"

The following can't be overstated: you **must** be reliable. Your job is to make your bosses' lives easier. They must be able to rely on you. If you're unreliable you can't possibly make their lives easier. Practise this behaviour with your family and friends to make it part of who you are. Your boss must feel that they can count on you.

You may be part of a bigger project that relies on each person doing the right thing, doing it accurately and doing it on time. Someone unreliable can cause all sorts of problems – which can be irritating or very costly for your employer. I remember when I used to do a lot of filming – the one thing that was drummed into me from day one was never ever be late because you were part of a very expensive team. And if you were late, the money being paid to everyone else was being wasted while there was a delay.

Don't think that a few minutes don't matter. They do matter. Just because it's not important to you, doesn't mean it's not important to an employer.

Being reliable costs nothing but it makes a huge difference in how you will be perceived and how professional you will be seen to be. And it's one of the most common criticisms I've heard from employers when they hire young people.

If you're new to the working world, making sure that you are professional and reliable is essential, if you want to be taken seriously.

Get this right and you will stand out in a very positive way. It doesn't matter how good you are if you're not there. It's as simple as that.

> *"Don't try to be like men in work. Be aware that as a woman, sometimes you have to be three times better in order to get the same respect as your male colleagues. Don't get upset and waste energy on that. Just stay calm and carry on.*
>
> *"Some men will try to intimidate you, in order to make themselves look better. In the end – they don't succeed. I've learned that the more they show this behaviour, the more afraid they are of you or your skills. Stay nice, just keep some distance from these guys.*
>
> *"At work it's good to compare yourself to a river. Sometimes you have to be like the water, going with the stream easily navigating through the rocks, stones and waterfalls. Sometimes slow, sometimes quick; be liquid like water. And sometimes you have to be like the rock, letting the water flow over you and not be affected by those currents."* Katrien Van der Veere

Maybe you're someone who likes to party. Great. I'm

not suggesting you don't. However, if you show up for work looking bedraggled or being exhausted you cannot possibly do a good job. Your ability to concentrate will be affected. Your energy level will be lower than normal. Your employer is paying for you to function at 100%. If you're barely awake or hung over, you can't do that. You don't deserve to be paid in full if you're not delivering in full.

Here's something else you need to be aware of that will also help you to score massive points with a client or an employer: showing initiative. Doing what needs to be done, rather than only doing what you've been told to do.

This requires you to think about what you're doing – at all times. And thinking about the needs of your employer. Imagine what it's like to be your manager – what would they do, expect or want you to do if something unexpected happened?

It's amazing how many people behave like unthinking robots – completely disengaged or disinterested in what they're doing and why they're doing it. A lot of people simply don't use common sense. It's as if they left their brains at home. To look at situations from your employers' perspective is very highly valued – and will cause you to act in ways that will set you apart from the others . . . in a positive way.

job interviews

An employer has a need. They need help and are busy people who would not waste their time asking to see you if they thought you were not a possible candidate for the job. All you have to do is show them that in choosing you, they will have made the right choice.

To get the result you want, you must understand fully what they want and then tailor what you say, how you look and how you behave to match it completely. Interviews are like performing in a play – for both the interviewee and the interviewer. No professional actor would perform without preparation and rehearsal. An amateur certainly can't afford to go into such a situation without doing at least some preparation.

When you walk into the interview, the interviewer will genuinely want to feel that in meeting you, the right candidate has been found. Most interviewers want an easy life, so make it easy for them – gently take the lead. This does not mean rushing in as 'personality of the month'. Aim for quiet self-confidence. Look upbeat, stand up straight and be friendly. They want to see if you'll fit in with their other workers.

Tell yourself that you can help them. Even though you may feel nervous inside, it's highly unlikely that the interviewer will know this. Use the interviewer's name – if you did not catch it, ask again. You will appear more confident using his or her name, and he or she will like it. As a young person it will usually be appropriate for you to show the respect associated with using the interviewer's last name and title (Mr, Ms, Dr, etc), but some industries or organisations are less formal and may use first names. Follow the lead of the interviewer.

Maintain eye contact; don't look nervously at the floor. When asked to talk about yourself don't blurt everything out; keep it brief, upbeat and relevant. You'll almost certainly get asked, *"What are you interested in?"* You must have an answer for that question. And you must sound enthusiastic about what you tell them. Rehearse beforehand so you don't 'um' and 'er' too much.

As part of your preparation find out as much as possible about the company. This can be done from their website. Speak to a few people who work there about what they do. Learning a lot about what the company does, how it fits into its industry, and how well it is doing will help to indicate your interest and seriousness.

To make a good impression, you should use this

information throughout the interview. But do not make the common mistake of blurting it all out at once. Use the knowledge to formulate lots of intelligent questions about the company. Have them on a piece of paper if necessary. You can turn a one-sided interview into a two-way conversation. This is a technique you can and should use. Even for entry level positions you can make a good impression by asking questions reaching far beyond the immediate job position. Gently weave into the conversation some of the questions below. They could also be of use at the end of the interview, when you will often be asked if you have any further questions:

- Who are the biggest competitors and how are they doing?
- What are the key challenges the company is facing at the moment?
- How proud are you to work for this company? Why?
- What is the company doing to cut its costs?
- What is being done to grow the business?
- How would you describe the management style or culture of the company?
- If you could change anything about the company, what would it be?

What you are trying to discover is how open, forward-thinking and realistic they are. Is the company thinking in the past or the future? By asking leading questions, you will also demonstrate how well informed you are. In some ways the answers you receive are unimportant.

During the interview, concentrate on issues relating to their needs rather than just your own. They are looking for someone to fill their needs, not someone who just needs a job.

When you know that the interview is coming to an end, gently take control by asking if there is anything else the interviewer would like to know about you. If not, thank them for the opportunity to meet and ask when you can expect to hear from the company. Most people don't ever think to ask for the job. So finish with, *"I'd really like to have this job. I am sure I can be helpful and do a great job for you."*

If you still can't get a job, create your own by becoming self-employed.

You can download a free audio course *How to Earn* from www.TheSensibleUncle.com/howtoearn. It will remain free for as long as our Internet web host doesn't charge us if a lot of downloads take place. So get in early.

what I wish I'd known about:

money

> "Save! Value your credit like you would value your reputation. Don't allow anyone else to take control of your money (not a friend, boyfriend, or husband). Always know what's happening with your finances." Kimberly Gauthier

Six millionaires and multi-millionaires have contributed their philosophies about money and checked this chapter for accuracy. This is information about money that rich people know about, but poor people usually don't.

Banking on marrying a rich guy isn't a sensible financial plan. As a woman, your earning potential has never been better, especially if you ever become a successful entrepreneur, as more and more women are discovering.

The biggest mistake you can make about money is taking advice from people who don't actually have much of it. Those people often go through their entire lives looking for the ways to 'get rich quick'. And fail.

Genuinely rich people on the other hand, tend to get rich **slowly**. Their wealth is accumulated over a very long period. And, contrary to what you may think from seeing celebrities in the media, the vast majority of rich people do not live a lavish lifestyle. They are rich because they keep their money – they don't waste it on expensive designer labels. They are particularly careful with money. That's precisely why they have so much of it.

You can't be a high spender and become a millionaire at the same time. Who is better off? A high earner who spends it all each year, or someone who earns less, but invests some of it wisely? It isn't the first person.

Be different. Quietly adopt the behaviours of those

who know the secrets of becoming wealthy and financially secure. The earlier you decide to copy what genuinely wealthy people do, the more you are likely to benefit in the long term.

Think of your future life as one of those colanders used to drain cooked vegetables. By the time you reach old age, it's highly likely that you will have earned a few million (pounds, dollars, euros or whatever) over many years. All that money was poured into your colander. But the question is, how much of it will you manage to keep, and how much will flow directly through it, down the plughole?

We're all so obsessed by money but just the mention of it can induce a glazed expression of utter boredom on most people's faces. Therefore, before you lose interest, do the following now and for the rest of your life. The next couple of paragraphs may be the most important in this book. If you are serious about building a healthy financial future, consider this very seriously indeed. If you only adopt one idea from this book – make it this:

Dear Daughter
From today, save 15% of everything you ever earn for the rest of your life.

One multi-millionaire who read this said, *"I disagree. Make it 20%."* No matter how much or how little money you earn – set aside this money before you do anything with your pay cheque. In other words 'pay yourself first'. This is important. Don't fool yourself into believing that you'll be able to pay yourself last. Human nature being what it is, you'll have spent it.

This 15–20% of everything you ever earn is not spending money. It must never be used to pay for day-to-day expenses or things like holidays. This 'capital' should only ever be invested to generate more money. Because you are young, you have something going for yourself that older women don't have, and that's time. Earlier we discussed how rich people get rich slowly. That's what you're looking to do. Money that you put away for forty years will earn you far more than money put away for only twenty. Or ten. The sooner you decide to adopt this 15–20% habit, the more likely you'll benefit longer term.

Capital is used to generate additional money. This income or interest is then added to the original capital. The increased capital is then capable of earning even more money, which is again added to the capital. This is the effect of compound interest. Compound interest, over a very long time, will help you become wealthy.

Experienced, smart investors use their capital to invest in a range of different ways. Some are very safe investments which generally deliver lower incomes, while other investments may be riskier. To compensate them for the risk they are taking, they hope to generate higher rates of return for their money. Because of the risks, they could lose their investment too. The combination of high and low risk investments is called their portfolio. A well-balanced portfolio will strike the best balance between the level of risk the investor is prepared to take with the income they receive from those investments. You can do this yourself if you are particularly knowledgeable or you can entrust the role to a professional adviser – who you have to choose very carefully indeed. They absolutely must be someone who is a) licensed and b) works for your best interests, not their own.

Genuinely rich people (as opposed to those who just want to appear rich) invest their capital in a variety of different ways to create various streams of income, which, when added together, allows them to live comfortably from that income.

They no longer have to work for a living. Their money now works for them instead. In contrast, most 'ordinary' people are only a few months' salary away from bankruptcy. Don't allow yourself to become one of those people.

By adopting this simple and profoundly effective financial habit from a young age, you will also learn financial self-discipline and responsibility. You will learn to use money to your advantage, rather than allowing yourself to be one of the hundreds of millions who hand over their hard-earned cash every week to make others even richer than they are already.

In our image-obsessed society, poor people tend to spend a high proportion of money they don't have on stuff they hope will make them look wealthy and successful. When they do this over a long period, they practically guarantee they'll stay poor.

Therefore, the first thing to realise is that being financially successful throughout your future life is all about how much of your money you keep. It's absolutely not about how much you spend, or the overpriced designer labels you spend it on. Decide from today to make it a lifelong priority to keep more of your money.

what you must know about debt

Poor people are either forced, or they allow themselves far too easily, to go into debt, and end up having to pay out a lot more in the longer term. Slavery may have been abolished hundreds of years ago in the West. But it's back. And it's spelt D.E.B.T. Debt really is a cruel form of slavery.

Each time you accept debt of any type, you are effectively allowing someone to tie a long chain around your ankle fastened to a heavy weight. The more you need that money, the shorter and tighter that chain is clamped. The shortest and heaviest chains are owned by your government. They spell 'debt' as T.A.X. For that, you have no choice. We are all indebted to our governments. In return, they use this money in a variety of ways. First, they pay the interest on mind-boggling, eye-watering levels of debt they usually blame the previous government for.

What's left funds lots of essential and some non-essential public services, our schools and public hospitals, pays state pensions to men and women who have been making contributions for many decades, and, of course, provides the funding for a military to defend (and in some cases to do far more than just defend) your nation.

Once we have paid our taxes, we are then free to spend whatever we have left in any way we choose. Although that's not strictly true, as we'll discuss a bit later. Anyone who feels that they don't have enough money left over to enjoy their life at the level they think they deserve, will 'choose' or allow themselves to spend now with someone else's money, and pay it back later. In other words, to go into debt.

When you go down Debt Road (probably in a car you've bought on credit), your life is under the control of those who own all the money you are borrowing.

Banks and credit card companies will fall over themselves to lend you money. They are particularly eager to lend money to students. They really want you to be in debt to them – from the earliest possible age. And they have miles and miles and tonnes of heavy chain at the ready for weighing you down with debt.

Realise this, an 'offer' of credit (the opportunity to go into debt) – is actually a request that could end up costing you a lot of money for many years. Banks and credit societies are not charitable organisations: you will be paying a lot for the privilege of spending right now. The interest you pay will substantially increase the total you spend. It may feel painless because each monthly payment seems low, but over time it all adds up – to a lot.

Therefore, do not go into debt unless you absolutely have to. The secret is to never find yourself in a situation where you have to go into debt at all. Although in reality that's almost impossible.

At some point, one of the biggest debts people take on is a mortgage on their home. What most don't realise is that you buy one home, but by the time you've made all the repayments, you've paid so much in interest that you've actually paid for more than two homes.In fact a lot of mortgage companies allow you to pay back the debt for a lot longer; twenty-five years instead of say, twenty years. You're made to think that they're doing you a favour with lower monthly repayments. What they're less keen to tell you is how much more interest you end up pay during those extra five years. And most of that interest gets paid in the first few years, when you barely pay off any of the actual loan.

One more money myth is the idea that a mortgaged home is your asset. It isn't. It's the bank's asset, not yours. They just give you permission to live there while you repay your loan. If you ever find that you can't repay the mortgage, the bank will take the home from you – potentially with all the cash you put into it, leaving you with nothing. A mortgage in your name is one of the shortest and strongest chains you will ever be shackled to.

Anyone who knows a lot about money will say there is such a thing as 'good' debt. That's outside the scope of this chapter. But even the experts make massive mistakes. The global economic meltdown in recent years is a brilliant example of how debt can bring down seemingly invincible financial institutions, even countries.

credit cards

The moment you're legally old enough to have a credit card, you'll receive invitations to have them. But if debt is so bad – should you get a credit card? Definitely yes. In fact, there is a strong case in favour of having two credit cards: one for work-related expenses, the other for personal use. And if you ever lose one, you'll have a backup. But never more than that. Forget store cards and charge cards. They can be extremely expensive ways to borrow money.

However, when you have credit cards, never use them for credit purposes. The money you borrow from credit card companies is very expensive indeed. Only use credit cards for convenience. Pay off the balance in full on each card every month. This can be done automatically. Set it up with your bank. Credit card companies know that millions of card holders forget to pay by the due date each month – so they make a fortune from interest they charge per day on the outstanding balances.

An additional benefit of having credit cards and paying them off in full each month is how it improves your credit rating. This may not seem important to you right now, but one day it will be. You will almost certainly need to arrange some kind of loan in the future. By building a track record of being a responsible card user, you'll increase the likelihood of being granted a loan as well as ensuring that your future credit rating doesn't suffer if you're refused.

In short, build up your capital. Reduce or eliminate debt. And do it all for a long time. Is this possible? Yes. But you need to know who and what is trying to stop you. And how they so cleverly persuade you to dip into your pocket for them – so often.

being a cash crop

Today everyone is bombarded with countless messages every day in an effort to persuade us to give in to temptation; to buy that chocolate bar or to spoil yourself with that new designer label. The human species has never had to face this much persuasion before. It's all designed to stop you from delaying gratification. And if you can't afford it right now – no problem. You can pay quickly and easily using a credit card. Now you know why you have to give your credit card details only once to companies like Apple. We've been persuaded to give them a backstage pass to our bank account. You can now get as many apps and music tracks immediately without ever thinking that you have to pay for them. How cool is that? For them it really is. And very profitable. Not only that, each time you buy something you tell them just a little bit more about what you like. That information is worth potentially more to them than how much you spend with them.

In the 1920s, for the first time in human history, factory production in the United States outstripped real demand. The population had to be persuaded to buy more so those factories could operate at full capacity and make the most profit. Companies came to realise that genuinely happy people didn't feel the need to buy much 'stuff'. That's not good for business. So what began was the development of the dissatisfied consumer. During the 20th century, women were the primary target for advertisers. Are you feeling plain and frumpy? Buy our clothes. Look like a film star, buy our cosmetics. One cosmetics company described their products as 'hope in a jar'. Hiring behavioural psychologists, marketers have learned precisely how to make women feel insecure, unloved or unappreciated. Women are then far more likely and willing to buy whatever it is they have to sell. Any idea why shopping is now called retail therapy?

Every waking hour for the rest of your life, you will be bombarded with opportunities to spend small or large amounts of whatever you earn. It's no accident that 'convenience stores' as so widespread.

It has become way too easy not to think about what you spend your money on.

Therefore, for one month decide to write down every single thing you spend money on. Do it every day for a month. You will probably get a shock when you discover how you are persuaded to fritter money away without even realising it. A lot of that money could have easily been used to boost your capital account.

Your ability to delay gratification is incredibly important if you are serious about building up capital. If your 'will power' consistently overpowers your 'won't power', you'll never get rich.

Therefore it is worth learning to delay gratification. Every time you stop yourself from spending money unnecessarily, you reduce your chances of going into debt and simultaneously free up money to be added to your capital.

"Don't ever compare yourself with anyone else. If you absolutely have to, compare yourself with those who have less than you, not more."
Sally Helvey

what I wish I'd known about:

decision-making

Being taught how to make better decisions isn't very common. Usually we're left to figure it out for ourselves and learn from our mistakes. There is a better option. In this section you'll learn a few techniques that will help you make more good decisions and fewer bad ones. Please note: this does not mean you will never make bad decisions. You will. Hopefully none of them will be fatal, have long-term consequences or be financially crippling.

Here's how to practically guarantee making **bad** decisions:

- Only consider your short-term needs.
- Only consider the needs of others.
- Only consider how you feel about the situation.
- Ignore the facts.
- Confuse facts with your own assumptions and/or the opinions of others.
- Fall for the 'This once-in-a-lifetime offer is only available for a limited time – buy now or miss out.' Don't allow yourself to be pushed into making decisions in this way.

Avoid the list above and you'll make more good decisions. In addition to the above, do more of the following.

Decide to decide things. This in itself is a decision and it builds your confidence. Not making a decision can be a bigger mistake than making bad decisions.

Understand how you currently make decisions. For example, what factors would you consider when choosing which college or university to apply for? The reputation of the institution and/or the tutors? How many years the course is? How near or far it is from home? Whether it is in the centre of a large city, or a quieter backwater campus? How vibrant the social scene is? Etc.

All these factors are important, but the interesting question to ask yourself is: how much importance do you give each of the factors relative to each other? And how likely is it that the way you tend to evaluate situations will lead to a better decision and to a good longer-term outcome? What might the consequences be if you gave certain aspects of your decision too much importance, or not enough?

From now on, after each decision you make, whether it's big or small, evaluate whether it was a good decision or not. This habit will help improve your 'hit rate' of good decisions. If you find that you are making a lot of decisions you later regret, it can be incredibly useful if you can learn how to uncover any recurring reasons. It could be that you tend to make many decisions too quickly, without thinking through possible or likely consequences. Or, on the contrary, maybe you agonise over every possible possibility, getting stuck in analysis paralysis. Then again, perhaps you are too afraid of what other people think, so you dither over all decisions. Learning to understand your decision-making strengths and weaknesses is a key skill.

Going along with decisions made by others can appear the easy option. In many cases, however, you pay a high price later. So, actively make more of your own decisions and accept responsibility for them. Caring parents may offer to bail you out if you make poor decisions. This is very loving of them, but be aware that knowing they are there as a safety net all the time can lead you to making ill-informed decisions because you are not ultimately responsible for the outcome. The sooner you decide to take full responsibility for your decisions, the sooner you'll take your decisions more seriously. Before you make future decisions learn these habits:

Stop. Step back. Look at the bigger picture. Define the situation. How important is this decision in the short and the longer term? If it's not that important, don't waste too much time evaluating all the options. Ask yourself, *"What else is worth considering?"*

If you can, step into the shoes of any other people who may or will be affected by your decision. If appropriate, ask them for their views or what they want. A great question to ask others is, *"If you were me, what would you do?"* Then ask, *"Why?"* Tell them you'll consider their position but you need to weigh up all the options before you make your decision. Accept now that not all decisions will be received well by everyone else.

As you'll find in years to come, the mark of a leader (even if you are only leading your own life) is the ability to make wise decisions that may be particularly unpopular in the short-term. So clarify your purpose. What do you want to achieve? What are the top priorities, what are the factors that are less important? What are the options you haven't yet thought about? Balance your personal well-being and factor in the importance of your decision to others. Don't only do what's right for you every time. Or what's right for others all the time.

Tossing a coin is not the way to run your life, so here is a technique you can use for a wide range of decision-making situations.

pros and cons

Take a sheet of paper. Draw a vertical line down the middle. On one side of the page list all the pros (positives). In the other column list all the cons (negatives). Simply doing this exercise might help you see in black and white what the decision needs to be. If you are still unclear, assign a number from 0 to 10 to each item you have written. The higher the number, the more important it is to you. Then count up all the numbers in each column. Before you make your final decision, take a second look at your scores. Have you based them on facts, opinions or preferences? Understanding this can have a significant impact on your final decision.

It's worth giving a special mention to the role your emotions play when making decisions. The better you understand your emotions, the more likely it will be that your decisions will be made from a firm and stable foundation. This is another reason why you need to strengthen your Emotional Core, as described on pages 28 to 69.

The next chapter focuses on your attitude towards risk. Risk is an integral part of how you make decisions. It is always worth giving some serious thought about the real and imagined risks associated with your decisions. Do you tend to ignore, overestimate, or underestimate risks? To ignore risk is potentially dangerous. What will, or what could, be the consequences to you or others when making risky decisions?

Ultimately, your life story will be the result of all the decisions that you ever make and those you don't. Therefore, it is worth learning from the earliest age how to increase the proportion of good decisions you make, and minimising your bad ones. On a personal note, I really wish I'd known how to do this stuff much earlier in my own life. It would have made so many things so much easier.

what I wish I'd known about:

risk, responsibility and reputation

Dear Daughter
Learn to evaluate all risks accurately. Be bold,
but not foolish. Go ahead, ask him out. Apply for
that dream job.

risk

How you make decisions, your ability to delay gratification (remember the marshmallow experiment mentioned earlier) and how addicted you are to the rush of adrenaline associated with risky behaviour are all linked. Taking risks can be exciting. The buzz can be quite addictive. It gives you the feeling that you're so alive, living on the edge.

However, each time you take a reckless risk and get away with it you strengthen your belief that the risk was actually low. This can escalate recklessness, until one day your luck will run out. What you came to believe was low risk, wasn't.

Just because you believe a risk is low, it does not mean you are correct. An obvious example: hundreds of thousands, if not millions, of young women throughout history have ended up with an unwanted pregnancy. How many of them thought *"It won't happen to me."* But it does happen all the time. When you are young, you are at your most fertile. It is therefore relatively easy for the majority of young women to get pregnant, especially if they are not being as careful as they could. Unprotected sex is a very high risk behaviour. Especially for a woman who has never given any serious thought to the longer-term consequences of an unwanted pregnancy. Sad to say, it's very possible a man will abandon a pregnant woman if being a father wasn't part of his plan. Going ahead with the birth of a child on your own will change your world for ever. And close down so many other opportunities open to you as a young woman.

I once had a light-hearted conversation with a female friend. I think we were joking about life and being a good person. She said, *"I don't think I'm a good person."* *"You're being too hard on yourself,"* I said. *"At least you've never killed anyone!"*

She paused and in a quiet voice said, *"I have killed someone. When I was young I had an abortion."* What followed wasn't a light-hearted conversation any more. You don't want to experience the emotional pain she endured.

A sign of a person's maturity (at whatever age) is how much thought they are prepared to give to the consequences of their actions. Mature people are prepared to accept full responsibility for what ever they do. And never blame others when things don't turn out well.

Most men and women in prison today are there not necessarily because they are bad people (although obviously a lot of them are), they're there because they have a really poor ability to assess risk. They either believed they would never get caught, or they simply didn't worry about it. Many never stop, even for a moment, to think about any possible consequences to their behaviour. That's fine if they are the only people who are affected by their behaviour. They will be the only ones to pay the price. When it affects innocent people, it can literally wreck lives.

Accept that everything has an element of risk. Never get in the way of a learning experience. But be safe, without wrapping yourself up in so much cotton wool you smother yourself. Accept that bad things sometimes happen. It's called life.

"I would tell my teenage self to take more risks and that failure only happens if you don't learn from those risks. Take the unknown class, go on

*that skiing trip despite never having skied, go
visit that new city or museum even if you have to
do it alone. I missed out on so many experiences
because I was afraid to try, and I think a lot of
teenage girls have the same fears."*
Emily Trower-Young

responsibility

Why bother being responsible? Why not do whatever
you want, whenever you want? Why pay money to learn
to drive? Why pay all that money to get insurance? Why
not take the risks?

Here's why: being responsible is at the centre of being a mature person. It starts with taking full responsibility for your own actions. And all the consequences
and rewards that go with that. Professionally, your ability to accept responsibility will be a key factor in your
career success. If or when you ever have a family, you'll
be responsible for the lives and well-being of your children. Therefore, you may as well get as much practice
at being responsible from today.

reputation

I was fifteen. My dad needed to give me another talking to
because I'd said something horrible to my mother (sorry
mum). As ever, I wasn't particularly interested in what he
was telling me. It was a waste of time for both of us. Then
he said something which hit me between the eyes. I remember it so clearly, it's as if it was yesterday. He told me
that it takes years to build a reputation and only moments
to lose it all. He said that our personal reputation was the
only thing we have. And added an almost throwaway remark, *"I can walk into any room anywhere, confident in
the knowledge that I will never meet anyone I have ever
cheated or mistreated. That allows me to sleep at night."*
Will you be able to say the same thing?

Times have changed since then. In this age of smart-phones and digital cameras, there's always someone on-hand to instantly record and 'pass on' evidence of 'bad behaviour'. Sometimes to millions via sites like YouTube.

Suppose you were applying for an amazing job. You really want that job. What would the potential employer see you getting up to if they searched for photos, videos and comments in places like Facebook? Employers and recruiters do that. They want to know what type of person you are in private, too.

A reputation is the complex result of all the decisions you make (and don't make), what others say about you behind your back, what they are prepared to say about you to influential people on your behalf, how much you are trusted, whether others perceive you as someone who is only interested in what's 'in it for you' or whether you are someone who is occasionally or regularly prepared to go out of your way to help others.

A good reputation will open more doors of opportunity for you. And is based on your character and integrity, which is all about what you do when no one is watching.

Dear Daughter,
Pause. Weigh up all the possible consequences, evaluate the risk – and always protect your reputation.

what I wish I'd known about:

woman power

As a woman you have so many resources at your disposal to exert your power. Some are obvious, others are far more subtle. They all have the potential to be an awesome resource for you. You can harness your power or you can squander it. It's important to understand true power: who has it, who doesn't and what you can do to ensure others don't exert their power at your expense.

The next time you're among a group of people (including friends), look closely and see if you can figure out who has the most (or the least) power. Remember what was discussed in an earlier chapter about 'pecking orders'.

Powerful, influential people are great observers. They understand the subtleties of people, their strengths, weaknesses and insecurities. They recognise the dynamics within groups. They know who has influence, who doesn't, and who **thinks** they have it. And they quietly use their observations to exercise and enhance their own power.

Of course there is always the potential to misuse power to manipulate others. How you acquire and use power and influence will determine what sort of woman you become. That's up to you.

The definitive book on understanding power and influence is *The 48 Laws of Power* by Robert Greene and Joost Elffers. Understanding this from an early age can be enormously beneficial to you professionally as well as personally. On the next page are just some of the factors that they have found affect your ability to exert power and influence.

Make the boss look good. Don't ever try to outshine him/her. Never let everyone know your intentions. Say less than you need to. Know more than you share with others. Take your reputation very seriously indeed. Develop it through your actions and the company you keep. Guard it. It's all you have. Be worth talking about (for positive reasons). Stand out. Draw people to you. Don't be known as someone who chases after others (including chasing after men.).

Avoid miserable or unhappy people. When you want help, realise that others respond better if there's something in it for them. Don't appeal to their mercy or gratitude. Know when to leave. People with the least power tend to stay to the end. Be unpredictable. Be very careful who you commit to. Never appear rushed. Always remain calm. Once you make a decision, be bold. Cultivate the appearance that your achievements were easy for you. No one needs to know how hard you work. Always appear less smart than you are.

If you have concluded that power isn't important to you – you'd better get used to not having any.

"When you don't have a plan, you become part of someone else's." Anonymous

what I wish I'd known about:

negotiating

No life skill has more potential to improve your personal power than an ability to negotiate: lower prices, better deals and more favourable terms. We all negotiate every day whether it's with family members, school friends or work colleagues. So it makes sense to understand how negotiating works.

When you know this process, you can become extremely skilful relatively quickly. And the benefits are not only immediate (for example, you pay less for the items you buy), they also help improve your reputation and success for the rest of your life. In short, you can seriously improve your life by knowing how to negotiate.

The skills you use as a good negotiator are useful in many other spheres of life too: confidence building, social skills, being more cooperative and gaining a more accurate understanding of the intentions and motivations of others.

First, let's dispel a myth about negotiating. It is not about being so tough you crush your enemy by extracting every penny from a deal. That's win-lose negotiating: I win, you lose. It happens (and some will try it on you sometime) but it isn't that effective. Win-win: 'I win and so do you' negotiations are far more preferable. Your ability to find a 'better way' is the mark of a skilled negotiator.

Negotiating can be extremely complex, but in this section we'll cover some of the basics about getting lower prices on the stuff you buy and how to persuade people to give you more of what you want, and be happy to do so.

I recently found myself needing a hotel room. I didn't have a reservation. At the reception desk, I ended up paying just half what it should have cost. Earlier this morning I called my insurance company to renew a policy. I was offered interest-free credit. Within two minutes I received a £60 discount instead of the credit. Another time I was buying a sports car, and with some coaching by the UK TV presenter and motoring journalist Jason Dawe I ended up saving £3,500. Not bad for twenty minutes work. I was more than happy to take Jason out for lunch afterwards as a 'thank you'. I didn't even mind him having a pudding.

After he explained the negotiating process to me, it was miraculous to see how it unfolded exactly as he'd predicted. My secret weapon for all of the above negotiations was this: I just asked for a discount!

It was as simple as that: learn the following words and use them whenever you get the opportunity: *"What's the best price you can offer me?"* In so many cases this one sentence alone will either get you a lower price instantly, or it opens up a conversation which leads you towards a better deal.

Think of the quoted price simply as the most the seller expects to receive. All you have to do is find out the least they are prepared to accept.

what it takes to negotiate

Before you engage in any negotiations there are a number of ideas it helps to be aware of. First and foremost: initially it takes courage. Don't be intimidated. Adopt the mindset that negotiating can be fun. Because it is. Even though everybody negotiates all the time, there's a widespread unspoken belief in the West that there's something a bit tacky about haggling. Put those thoughts out of your mind. Effective negotiations are conversations. Bad negotiations are usually arguments.

Good negotiators are always professional, calm, polite, friendly and respectful. Why? Because it always helps you get a better deal. No one wants to give concessions to people who are rude, angry and unreasonable. This is fundamental to effective negotiation. As your skill and confidence grows, you will gain far more respect and you'll get better outcomes.

This point is absolutely critical: know what you want. It's amazing how many people are prepared to negotiate but have no idea what their preferred outcome is. Think about it before you start negotiating. Ask yourself what you must have, what would be great to have, what you'd be prepared to settle for and what you refuse to accept. Where is the 'wiggle room'? What are the points you are prepared to discuss and what is not negotiable? But be flexible.

Know what the other person wants, too. By understanding the intentions and motivations of others, you can use that knowledge to get a better deal for yourself. Never decide or guess what they are prepared to accept – ask them. Then focus on the gap between what you each want and see if you can find a way to get what you want as well as allow them to get what they want. Sometimes this requires a bit of creative thinking. The objective is to work with them not against them. Work together to reach a solution that is good for both of you. Help them to feel good about negotiating with you. It doesn't have to be unpleasant.

If a company has genuinely let you down or given you poor service, provide a detailed explanation of how they failed you. Pause. Let the other person speak. Don't interrupt. Pause again and then calmly ask, *"What are you prepared to offer me as compensation?"* Because you've thought about it ahead of time, politely tell them what you think would be fair.

All of this preparation can have a massive effect on the outcome of a negotiation. By thinking it through beforehand, you are less likely to have to think on your feet, which can be difficult.

Know when to shut up. After you've discussed the deal, make your considered offer. Then stop talking. Let the other person own the 'embarrassing silence'. This is what professional salespeople do to potential customers. They know it gets a lot of people to say *"yes"*. Be aware when it's being done to you.

Don't ever let the seller know how much you want something. It weakens your position.

Understanding your position in a negotiation is essential. For example, if you're buying the latest 'must-have' fashion, your position is weak. The seller can afford not to negotiate, confident that the next buyer will pay full price. Whereas if someone is selling because they have a monthly sales target to reach and it's the last day of the month, your position is much stronger.

Before you ever buy an expensive item, it is essential that you do your research ahead of time. Search the Internet for prices, specifications and model numbers. Know what you're talking about. Print out the best deals. Take them with you. Make sure you're comparing like-for-like products. Having printed materials with you will carry far more weight in a negotiation than merely saying you've seen a better price 'somewhere'.

If you're dealing with a salesperson, printed comparisons help them to find ways to justify giving you a better price or terms. They can't just give you whatever you ask for as they are often answerable to a sales manager and need to be able to give a logical reason why they gave you the deal. When buying a high priced item, professional negotiators often respond in this way: they suck in air, purse their lips, pause and say, *"That's a lot more than I was expecting."* This is acknowledged as part of the negotiation dance. If a salesperson ever asks you *"What price did you have in mind?"* this is a clear sign that he or she is open to a discussion and knows that he/she is dealing with a negotiator. Game on!

Know when to walk away. And never allow your ego to keep 'fighting to win' when you also know that you don't want what's on offer that much.

You will eventually encounter unethical liars and cheats. Don't ever become one yourself. You really don't need to be when you know how to negotiate professionally. Maintaining your integrity will mean that people will trust you. Earn and deserve that trust. This has a substantial effect on your long-term reputation. We'll cover how to identify when you're the one being manipulated or deceived a little later.

These are useful negotiation questions for you to ask:

- *"Is that the best price you can offer me?"*
- *"What do you need, for this deal to work?"*
- *"What's negotiable? What isn't negotiable?"*
- *"I really like it, but this is all the money I've got."*

Each time you get what you want in a negotiation, you improve the likelihood that you will get a better deal the next time too. It doesn't have to be at the expense of other people.

The best place you can practise your negotiating skills is probably a local car boot or yard sale. Among the junk you will find absolute bargains. Few sellers ever expect a buyer to accept their asking prices, which may be rock bottom anyway. Everything is therefore negotiable. You can practise at very low cost. Why not go along with some friends? Decide on the maximum you are each allowed to spend and agree to meet up again in, say, thirty minutes to show each other what bargains you've managed to nab. Split up. Don't shop together in a group. And don't buy any stuff you don't want or need just because it was cheap.

Whatever savings you make from all your future negotiations, put the money you saved into your capital account as described in the money section. If you had paid full price for an item that money would have disappeared anyway – so put it to good use.

how to protect yourself

Paying lower prices is only part of what negotiating is about. Suppose you are asked to do something you don't want to do by a friend, your guy or family member. You don't have to go along with everything other people want all the time. Discuss alternatives at least sometimes. Being easy-going is admirable but you need to ensure that no one ever thinks of you as a pushover. Occasionally asking for something in return is reasonable.

If you're ever asked to do something significant 'out of the blue', this could be a ploy that isn't as spontaneous as it might appear. It's designed to destabilise you. It is often used by manipulative people to get their own way, at the expense of their 'victim'.

If you're ever put on the spot and don't know what to do about a request or an offer say, *"I'm open to your offer/idea. Tell me more about it before I make a decision."* This tells the person you're taking them seriously, but you are not prepared to commit to a decision too quickly. If you would prefer time to think about something further, say so. Don't allow yourself to get cornered into making decisions too soon.

Sometimes, you'll be set a time limit by the seller. If you feel pressured, simply walk away from the deal.

In business, I'm often asked this question: *"Are you prepared to negotiate your fees?"* My answer is often, *"Yes. You can pay me more."* They usually laugh and agree to my fee.

Being seen to negotiate is a sign that you are self-confident and assertive. If your negotiating style is aggressive you'll appear arrogant. Even though it might feel thrilling to negotiate like a 'tough guy', you'll often end up with a worse deal.

There is no better way to flex your power muscles than by learning the art of negotiation. The sooner you begin, the more power you will start to attract. Negotiation is a fascinating topic.

Study it to become an expert.

some final words

Please use all the information in this book as a spring-board for further knowledge on what it takes to be a woman. Don't agree with everything you've read. Discuss the most relevant topics with your family and friends.

Revisit topics. If you are a teenager, you are growing at a very fast rate; physically, intellectually and emotionally. What you thought about a wide range of subjects is probably very different now to what it was only six months ago. What isn't particularly relevant to you today may be incredibly important to you in just a few months time.

If you have found this book particularly helpful please tell your friends about it. And ask them to visit The SensibleUncle.com

Let's close with a few thoughts from two fabulous women. Jan O'Leary is seventy-six, the mother of four daughters. Here is just some of what she has learned about life as a woman:

- *Do not give sex to obtain 'love'.*
- *Male predators will say they love you to obtain sex.*
- *Beware of destructive females who will try to undermine nice people, especially when envious.*
- *Never hurt another person either physically or emotionally. Especially when you've convinced yourself they 'deserve' it.*
- *Remember that beauty shines through from your inner-self. The eyes reveal who you really are. If the beauty is within your soul, it will be reflected in your outward appearance.*
- *The colouring you are born with suits your individuality. Only ever enhance your skin, hair or eyes. Never try to change them.*

- *There are many different figure shapes and sizes; not one shape being the norm.*
- *If you ever have a baby, do your pelvic floor exercises following the birth. It will help the recovery of your figure and improve your sex life.*
- *Do not grow old wishing that you had taken better care of yourself.*

Kimberly Gauthier is an entrepreneur who runs her own online business (www.KimberleyGauthier.com).

"When I was a teenager, I felt powerless, always under the thumb of the adults around me. What I didn't realise at the time was that I did have the power to choose how I reacted. I didn't have to be a slave to my emotions. If I was able to talk to my young self, I'd tell myself the following:

"I wish I would have known how quickly my teen angst would vanish into a memory that I wouldn't care about. All the drama of being a teenager is a distant memory and often seems like a story I heard about. All the people I had conflict with went away, all the embarrassing moments were forgotten, and all the broken hearts are barely a memory.

"You don't know everything. Twenty years from now, you still won't know everything. So instead of being so unpleasant when someone gives you advice, actually consider what they're saying. No one owes you anything. Despite what you see your friends getting or what you see on television, no one is required to provide you with a lifestyle.

"If you don't take care of yourself first, then you're no good to anyone else. There's no point in maintaining relationships that hurt or cause stress.

"Emotions are a great guide to showing you if

you're on the right track or the wrong track. If you're feeling crappy, then you're on the wrong track. My self-esteem and happiness is all up to me!

"Don't ever look to others to make you feel valued or appreciated. When you get that from others, it's the icing on the cake, but not the cake. It's up to me to make myself feel valued and appreciated.

"Although we have to take care of ourselves first, we also need to understand that we owe it to the people around us to be in a good mood. Having a positive attitude raises everyone up. Being kind to people even when you're not feeling 100% will help you get to 100% that much faster.

"There are days when I don't feel like it, but sometimes a small smile is enough to spread kindness and project a nice attitude. We don't have to put on a fake face for others, we just need to avoid bringing them down.

"My favourite saying is that 'People come into our lives for A Reason, A Season, A Lifetime'. Learn something from each person who comes into your life. Show toxic people the door – don't give them any more energy than it takes to escort them out of your life. Instead, cherish and appreciate the great people.

"Stop wasting your time chasing after the 'love of your life' as a teen. In ten years, you'll barely remember his name and you'll have 'fallen in love' with many more guys. Instead of focusing on 'happily ever after', focus on making solid friendships.

"I wish I'd known that (1) girls need fathers and (2) a woman's goal isn't marriage, it should be happiness. If we find happiness in a relationship, great, but we shouldn't allow the quest to find a man rule our lives. Any man who makes you feel bad about yourself isn't worth your time.

Run! Don't give second chances. Run!

"Marriage doesn't ever have to be the next step. Just because you've been dating for five years doesn't mean you have to get married now. A relationship is going to have its ups and downs – don't pack a bag during a **down***. Learn from those moments, communicate, and get ready for the* **up** *to return.*

"If you're not in a stable, committed relationship, don't drag a child into your drama. If you don't want to have children, don't allow your family and friends to pressure you.

"Cherish female friendships. So many women are atrocious to each other. Don't be this type of woman. Even if you're not someone's biggest fan, don't become their enemy by tearing them down. As women, we need to support one another, even if that support is by choosing to be silent.

"Wash your face daily. Sleeping in your make-up not only kills your sheets, you age ten times faster.

"I truly believe that our thoughts and emotions create our reality, and I wish I would have known about the power of the Law of Attraction. I now always ask myself 'What am I attracting?' If I'm in a negative mood, then I'm attracting more negativity. When I'm frustrated, then I'm attracting more frustrating situations. When I'm happy, I'm attracting more happiness."

In closing, be the woman you want to be. Dress and behave exactly the way that suits your style and personality. This book has been a sincere attempt to guide you towards being the best version of who you choose to be as a woman. Enjoy the journey. The world needs far more self-assured, happy, independent and successful women. You are invited to be one of them.

thank you

Many men and women have contributed to this book. Thank you to all of you. Special thanks to the following:

Vanessa & Sarah Catrin Anderson; Lisa Bahar LMFT LPCC; Dianne & Claire Bendle; Stephanie Bennett of ProofScrutiny.co.uk; Trish Bertram; Anne Casey; Mary Ellen Ciganovich; Donna Cravotta; Fiona David; Jessica Drummond MPT, CCN, CHC; Reeva Dunning Putney; Lisa L Flowers; Maria Franzoni; Kimberly Gauthier; Chrissie Godson; Lara Goldman; Talor (Tippi) Hanson; Henry Harington; Hallie Hawkins; Sarah-Jane Hawkins; Sally Helvey; Deb Hulbert; Joanna Jones; Chris & Elloitt Kane; Adrienne Kirkman; Juli Klie; Sophie Leacacos, Meredith Lloyd; Heidi Smith Luedtke, PhD; Penny Mallitte; Jessie Marr; Shekinah Monee; Sally Palaian, PhD; Antony Parselle; Leslie Richin; Joe Robertson; Lyndsay Russell; Ashley Schwartau; Kari and Kylie Sellers; Sally, Julie, Michaela, Jill and Leah Sheppard; Peter Simonson; Kate Sturgess; Sherrie Tennessee MBA; Katrien Van der Veere; Emily Trower-Young; Julie Walsh; Sarah Jo Wood.

about the author

A former BBC reporter and news anchorman in London, England, Roy Sheppard is the author of numerous relationship books. He is often referred to as 'The Sensible Uncle' in the media. And brings people together in his role as a professional conference moderator for many of the world's largest and most successful organisations. As the 'conscience of the audience', he specialises in chairing complex and confidential discussions. Roy is also an experienced keynote speaker on the subject of relationships, networking, reputation, referrals and how to be upbeat in a downbeat world.
Visit: www.RoySpeaks.com for more information.

other books by roy sheppard

Dear Son: what I wish I'd known at your age. For all 15 to 25 year-old men.

How to Be The One. This book is about how to be a better girlfriend, boyfriend, husband or wife.

Meet, Greet & Prosper. Having hundreds of 'friends' you've never met on Facebook is one thing, but how do you start 'real' relationships? This pithy pocket book tells you all you need to know about turning strangers into friends. Also available as a **FREE** eBook.

www.TheSensibleUncle.com/MGP

That Bitch. Co-written with Mary T Cleary, this book provides detailed information to help men and women protect themselves against these deeply disturbed, dangerous women who often prey on particularly kind, gentle men and women.

Rapid Result Referrals. Practical ideas to generate more word-of-mouth and referral sales for your business.

To order these books, visit www.TheSensibleUncle.com

How to Be The One
Be a better girlfriend, wife, boyfriend or husband

"The self-help path to true love"
Mail on Sunday, YOU magazine

"This new book will teach you a whole new attitude - you'll be fighting the men off!"
More! Magazine

"How to be LOVED. Whether you're single, married, coming out of a relationship, or just want to get on with people better, this will help...an inspiring new book"
Bella Magazine